Mantle Ministry:

Catching the mantle of your Elijah

By
Bill Jamison

PASTOR OF THE VINEYARD CHURCH
NAVAL AIR STATION KEFLAVIK, ICELAND
1996 - 1999

Mantle Ministry: Catching the mantle of your Elijah

ISBN 978-0-9835320-1-9

Published by Prindle House Publishing
www.prindlehouse.com
PO BOX 18761
Jacksonville, FL 32229
866-877-4635

For bulk ordering and booking information please email customerservice@
prindlehouse.com

Printed in the United States of America

Dedication

I dedicate this book to my lovely wife Diane and our seven children, Sissley, Ruhamah, Joshua, Abria, Barakah, Leah and Aimee.

Much of what I have written about in this book was taken from my trials and errors as a husband and father. Because you have been inherent participants in my walk with God, I have gained some insights about leading and following that may be of value to others.

Acknowledgements

Mom and Dad - thanks for loving me and passing on to me the heritage of your faith in God.

Sister Gloria, Brother Norman, Sisters Betty, Harriett and Miriam, Brothers Steve and Matthias – Thank you for displaying your faith in God and steadfast love for me.

Joshua and Virginia Phillips - thanks for loving me unconditionally.

Joshua Phillips - thanks for being my Elijah and recognizing my potential in God.

Eddie and Hattie James - thanks for your long-standing friendship and abiding love.

Pastors George and April Davis - Thanks for leading me with superb leadership in the excellence of God's love.

Forward

I am honored to write this forward to Bill Jamison's first book entitled Mantle Ministry: Catching the Mantle of Your Elijah. It is a wonderful revelation and gift to the Body of Christ. To take a quote from the book, Mantle Ministry is truly "manna in a different manner". It is evident from the pages of this book that Bill has been in God's presence and has learned to feed himself from His Word; and now he is passing on what he has eaten to the Body of Christ in this book.

Without a doubt, Mantle Ministry is a unique revelation, and yet it is a prolific tool that God has given to the Body of Christ through Bill's thoughts and written words. It is also an effective tool for developing godly relationships between the young and old, because it lines up with the Word of God throughout every page.

I believe that Mantle Ministry is a valuable resource for all Christians regardless of their level of maturity. It is my prayer that Holy Spirit will direct it into the hands of all the Elijah(s) and Elisha(s) that are in the Kingdom of God today.

Gloria G. Jamison, Bible Teacher and Evangelist, Maranatha Faith Christian Center, Columbus, MS

Table of Contents

Chapter 1   THE REVELATION   1

Chapter 2   MANTLE MINISTRY   16

Chapter 3   THE MANTLE OF JESUS   28

Chapter 4   LEADERSHIP AND FOLLOW-SHIP   35

Chapter 5   GILGAL MINISTRY   43

Chapter 6   BETHEL MINISTRY   54

Chapter 7   JERICHO MINISTRY   61

Chapter 8   JORDAN MINISTRY   72

Chapter 9   MANTLE OF LOVE   88

Chapter 10   GETTING GOD'S BEST IN MINISTRY   97

Appendix   NOTABLE EXAMPLES OF BIBLICAL LEADERSHIP   102

Chapter 1

The Revelation

Ministering under the covering of another
Follow-ship that leads to Leader-ship

John the Revelator was on the Isle of Patmos when he received the New Testament Revelation from Jesus Christ. Moses was in the right location in the Sinai Desert when he saw the Burning Bush, heard the Voice of God and received his call from God to deliver the Children of Israel from Egypt. Elisha was with Elijah at the Jordon River when Elijah was taken away to heaven by the Chariot of Fire. Because of his location, he was able to catch Elijah's mantle when it fell.

William Thomas Dillard, the founder of the Dillard Department Store Chain, once said that "there are three important things one must acquire to be successful in business; they are location, location, location". I believe that location is one of the most important factors in any successful venture. With that said, I want to take the opportunity to share with you how God orchestrated my circumstances to get me in the right location to receive the revelation of Mantle Ministry.

1

THE MOVE SOUTH

In 1985 I resigned from the Bonneville Power Administration of Portland, Oregon to work with my two brothers who owned a construction company in Columbus, Mississippi. Bonneville was a government agency under the Department of the Interior at the time. Prior to my resignation, I had worked as a Project Manager in energy conservation for five years. I moved from Portland to Mississippi to work with my bothers as an Administrative Assistant for Construction Projects. It was a big change of pace for me but I was excited to be able to work with my brothers. It was an opportunity for me to return home, and to not only work in a Christian environment, but to be with my family as well.

After two years, things went further south than we wanted them to. We got into a lot of litigation over some contracts that had gone bad and ended up having to shut the business down. This left me without a job, with a wife and three children to take care of, and no construction skills to speak of, except for what I knew about construction administration. After some soul searching and discussion with my wife, I decided to move to Birmingham, Alabama, hoping to find employment in my field. Unfortunately, jobs where hard to come by in Birmingham, especially for an outsider. Instead of a job in my field, I ended up taking a job with another construction company as an Administrative Assistant. Within three months I was out of a job again, this time, for sixteen months. During those sixteen months I did odd jobs to put food on the table. Eventually, I went back to work with one of my brothers as a construction foreman in Aniston, Alabama.

At this time I did some deep introspection and reflection on the course of events that led to my current situation and decided that the best course for me was to try to get hired again as a government employee before I got too old to compete. So I applied for jobs with federal agencies everywhere I could. One day, as I was working as a foreman on a mall project for my brother, he came and said that he knew that I would be leaving soon, so he wanted me to train someone to do what I had been doing as foreman. At the time I was not thinking of getting a job elsewhere, I was just trying to be the best foreman I could be. Sure enough, a few days later I got a call from the Personnel Officer at the Naval Air Station in Meridian Mississippi, asking me if I wanted to take a position as the Deputy to the Commanding Officer for Equal Employment Opportunity for the Civilian Work Force. Of course, I was very excited about the offer and could hardly wait until she finished her sentence. To make a long story short, I was reinstated with the government at the same rank and level that I had prior to resigning from the Bonneville Power Administration in Portland, Oregon.

I settled into my new job and went off to training. At the training facility, I met a trainer who saw my potential in the field and asked if I would like to assist her in training projects in the future. I agreed to work with her. Over time, we developed a good working relationship. After my training was complete and I was well into my new job, I can recall sitting in my office and looking out the window and saying to myself, "This is not permanent; I will not stay here long."

THE DREAM

After being Deputy to the Commanding Officer for about three years, I had a dream. In the dream my trainer called me and asked if I would like to have dinner with her and someone she wanted me to meet. She told me that I needed to be on my Ps and Qs because we would be eating at an exclusively elegant restaurant. I agreed to dine and met her and her guest at the restaurant. Not only was it exclusively elegant, it was a revolving restaurant with a speaker's mound in the center of it. I had never seen anything like it. Her guest was a very intellectual looking man who was well dressed and spoke with a distinguished British accent. To say the least, I was nervous and did not know quite how to handle myself. I remember saying to myself that I had better make sure that I use the correct eating utensils and display good table manners while in his presence. I found myself rehearsing the table manners my mother taught me as a little boy. Up to this point, I had never had a need to be concerned about them, but boy I sure needed to be correct on this occasion.

We did the usual exchange of names and where-you-are-from routine, but I would only speak when spoken to. He did most of his talking to my trainer. Then all of a sudden, he got up and went to the speaker's mound and began speaking about the ecology. He was indeed eloquent and well spoken. He captivated the entire restaurant with his presentation, returned to the table where we were sitting and said to me, "Now it's your turn to speak at the mound."

I knew I had to come up with something very quickly, so I said to him, "All I know how to do is preach the Gospel." I went to the mound and preached the greatest salvation message I had ever heard, and returned to my seat. I got a standing ovation from the audience and could see that he was pleased with my preaching as well. The dream came to an end at this point.

Then Holy Spirit spoke to me about the interpretation of the dream. He said that the whole ordeal at the restaurant was my interview for a new job and that I would be working for a foreigner who is a very eloquent man. He said that the sermon at the mound was a precursor to my actually working in the ministry in a foreign land. He said that my purpose for going to the foreign land was to minister the Gospel there, but my job with the government was my ticket there; that I would be diligent on my government job and effective as a minister of the gospel during my time off the job. He also said that the eloquent man in my dream represented my having favor with my new boss who also had a favorable disposition toward my working in the ministry in his country.

MINISTRY IN ICELAND

Approximately two weeks after I had the dream, sure enough, I got a call from my trainer. She asked if I would be interested in moving to Iceland to work as Deputy to the Commanding Officer there. And she said, "Oh by the way, should you take this job, you will be working for an Icelander."

At that moment I knew right then and there that the assignment was of the Lord, because the person I would be working for was a foreigner, just as I had seen in the dream. So I went home and told my wife that I had been offered a job in Iceland; and what did she think about moving to Iceland? She said, without hesitation, "Let's do it."

Now, I know it's God when my wife responds like that without giving a lot of thought to the question. Within a month's time we had gotten passports and visas, and my wife, our five children and I moved to Iceland.

In Iceland I did indeed work for an Icelander who was a very eloquent man. He was a diplomat who knew how to manage the affairs of the Status Force Agreement between Iceland and the United States of America. He also saw me as an ambassador for

America and introduced me to many of his countrymen. He took my wife and me to an exclusively elegant, revolving restaurant in Reykjavik, Iceland. I was able to develop a good relationship with many of the Christians in Iceland. I ministered at many of their churches and many of my sermons were televised over the Icelandic Christian Television Net (ICTN). To this day, I still communicate and fellowship with some of my Icelandic Christian friends.

Iceland is known as the land of fire and ice. To me, fire and ice have always been a strange combination. I never understood how hail and fire could fall from the sky to the earth at the same time. They seem so opposite to each other. But from what I know about God, he can take seemingly opposite substances and cause them to work together. This is very evident in Iceland because it sits on a volcano, yet it has a very cold climate. Approximately 11% of Iceland's surface is covered by glaciers known as Vatnajökull, which is the largest glacial cap in Europe. Because there is a warm gulf-stream coming up to the South coast, the country is not as cold as its location suggests. But winters are long, with about two months where there is very little daylight. At the end of January the daylight gradually gains on the darkness. Around March 23, the equinox signals more daylight than darkness, until the middle of May. After all the darkness has gone, the country has continuous daylight for two months. It is during this time that you can see the Midnight Sun.

So it was in October of 1994 that we arrived at the U.S. Naval Air Station in Keflavik, Iceland and I assumed my duties as Deputy to the Commanding Officer for Equal Employment Opportunity. Keflavik is about 35 miles from Reykjavik, the Capital of Iceland. We lived on the Naval Installation for five and a half years and returned to the United States in February of 1999. We had an opportunity to experience Navy life as civilians. It was also an adventurous time for our family. We were able to travel around the country and learn more about the people, their culture and their land. We have many very fond memories of those golden days in Iceland.

Over the years, I have lived many places in the United States and abroad. In each place, I can recall a particular insight or revelation that I received from the Lord. But it was in Iceland, the land of fire and ice, that the Lord opened my eyes to what I call "Mantle Ministry". My move from Oregon to Mississippi and then to Iceland established the back drop for Mantle Ministry and ultimately put me in position to receive this revelation from the Lord.

The Origin of the Revelation

The context for Mantle Ministry is found in 2 Kings 2:1-15, but the concept of Mantle Ministry was born out of a situation where I had a lot of young military members attending Church who needed spiritual guidance. Many of them had just become Christians and others had been Christians for some time but had not been grounded in the Word of God because of their constant mobility. It was here that Holy Spirit revealed to me the concept of Mantle Ministry as a means of assisting young believers in their growth and maturity in Jesus Christ.

Thus, Mantle Ministry is a guide for training Christians to be good followers and ultimately good leaders, by applying the biblical principles found in 2 Kings 2:1-15 and related scriptures. It also highlights the father-son relationship and can be used as a manual for mentoring young men and women. There are four stages of Mantle Ministry; the Gilgal Stage, the Bethel Stage, the Jericho Stage and the Jordan Stage. Mantle Ministry starts with service that leads to promotion and ends in leadership with humility. Now, let take a closer look at 1 Kings 19:19-21 and 2 Kings 2:1-15 to establish our premise for what we will discuss in the preceding chapters.

1 *Kings* 19:19-21

19 *So he departed from there, and found Elisha the son of Shaphat, who was plowing with twelve yoke of oxen before him, and he was with the twelfth. Then Elijah passed by him and threw his mantle on him.*

20 *And he left the oxen and ran after Elijah, and said, "Please let me kiss my father and my mother, and then I will follow you." And he said to him, "Go back again, for what have I done to you?"*

21 *So Elisha turned back from him, and took a yoke of oxen and slaughtered them and boiled their flesh, using the oxen's equipment, and gave it to the people, and they ate. Then he arose and followed Elijah, and became his servant.*

From these verses, we can see that it is the leader who sees potential in a prospective follower. We see that Elijah initiates the relationship with Elisha by throwing his mantle on him. I believe it is incumbent upon leaders to recognize the potential leadership in those under them, and then take the necessary steps to initiate the ministry relationship.

In Numbers 11:16-17, God told Moses to choose seventy potential leaders from among the people and bring them to the Tabernacle. There He would walk with Moses among those he had chosen and take of the spirit that He had put on Moses and put it on them. Then they would help Moses bear the responsibility of leading the people. Notice that it was incumbent upon Moses to identify those who had potential for leadership and then God would certify them as leaders-in-training before the people. The key principle here is that God shows the leader whom he should chose to follow him.

But it is the responsibility of the followers to cut all ties with those things that hinder them from making a total commitment to ministry. We see what Elisha did in verse 21 above: "So Elisha turned back from him, and took a yoke of oxen and slaughtered them and boiled them, using the oxen's equipment, and gave it to the people, and they ate. Then he arose and followed Elijah, and became his servant".

An example of this is when I attended the Word of Faith Southeastern Bible Training Center in Jacksonville, Florida. I was told that I had to attend school during the day. There was no night school. It was that way on purpose. The Center was looking for people who could totally commit to ministry. If I could not attend day sessions, then that was the one indication that I was not ready for the school. Elijah was looking for this kind of commitment from Elisha.

Obviously, farming was something that Elisha enjoyed doing and he was very successful at it. When God calls you to ministry, you will probably be at the top of your game in some profession. Like Elisha, you will have to decide whether or not to answer the call. In Elisha's case, he first celebrated going into the ministry with his friends, using the very tools of his trade - the oxen and his farm equipment. In doing this, he was saying to God, to his friends and to himself; "I am taking what resources I have to launch myself into ministry; I am closing all doors to ever going back to what I used to do so that I can give myself fully to ministry."

This is the decision you should make if you want to be successful in developing the ministry that God has called you to. You should make this decision as a farmer does when he plants seed in the ground. He expects a return on the seed sown. In other words, all the resources you put into your growth in ministry will return to you, not only in double portion, but in thirty, sixty or even a hundredfold.

2 *Kings* 2:1-15

1 And *it came to pass, when the LORD was about to take up Elijah into heaven by a whirlwind, that Elijah went with Elisha from Gilgal.*

2 *Then Elijah said to Elisha, "Stay here, please, for the LORD has sent me on to Bethel." But Elisha said, "As the LORD lives, and as your soul lives, I will not leave you!" So they went down to Bethel.*

3 *Now the sons of the prophets who were at Bethel came out to Elisha, and said to him, "Do you know that the LORD will take away your master from over you today?" And he said, "Yes, I know; keep silent!"*

4 *Then Elijah said to him, "Elisha, stay here, please, for the LORD has sent me on to Jericho." But he said, "As the LORD lives, and as your soul lives, I will not leave you!" So they came to Jericho.*

5 *Now the sons of the prophets who were at Jericho came to Elisha and said to him, "Do you know that the LORD will take away your master from over you today?" So he answered, "Yes, I know; keep silent!"*

6 *Then Elijah said to him, "Stay here, please, for the LORD has sent me on to the Jordan." But he said, "As the LORD lives, and as your soul lives, I will not leave you!" So the two of them went on.*

7 *And fifty men of the sons of the prophets went and stood facing them at a distance, while the two of them stood by the Jordan.*

8 *Now Elijah took his mantle, rolled it up, and struck the water; and it was divided this way and that, so that the two of them crossed over on dry ground.*

Notice, at Gilgal Elijah tells Elisha to stay while he goes to Bethel. He then leaves Bethel and goes to Jericho, and from

Jericho to Jordan. Before he goes to each of these places he gives Elisha the choice of going with him or saying behind. This was a test of Elisha's loyalty and commitment to ministry. God is a "who-so-ever-will" God. He will never force you to do something against your will. He will always give you opportunities to leave the ministry during difficult times. This is His way of testing your loyalty and commitment to serving Him.

SERVING BY ANY OTHER NAME

At this point, we should define the word ministry. Some people have the idea that when you become a minister, you are placed into a special class of people in the church who gets special treatment. You should be looked up to, given a special place to sit, and everyone should honor and respect you. While there is nothing wrong with any of these things in their proper place, being a minister is first and foremost about serving others.

The Hebrew word for minister is "Sharath", which means to serve, a servant, one who provides a service, a servitor or one who waits on another. The earliest mention of the word minister in the Bible is found in Exodus 24:13, where it says … "And Moses rose up, and his minister Joshua: and Moses went up into the mount of God."

The Greek word for minister is "Diakonos", which means one who executes the commands of another, especially of a master or a king; a waiter, one who serves food and drink. Our word "deacon" is derived from the Greek word Diakonos.

The first mention of the word minister in the New Testament is found in Matthew 20:26, where Jesus is speaking to his disciples about serving. In the preceding verses, the mother of James and John (the Sons of Zebedees) came to Jesus and asked if He could ensure that her two sons received places of honor when he came into his kingdom.

In Mark's account, James and John themselves came to Jesus and asked that they be granted to sit, one on his right and the other on his left, when he comes into his kingdom. This started some discontent among the other disciples, and when Jesus got wind of it He took time to explain to them how things work in the kingdom of God. He told them that the position of honor was not his to give. Only His heavenly father could grant such a request, and that He had already granted it to those it should be granted to.

In Matthew 20:25 we see why Jesus found it necessary to address this issue with his disciples. "But Jesus called them [unto him], and said, Ye know that the princes of the Gentiles exercise dominion over them, and they that are great exercise authority upon them. But it shall not be so among you: but whosoever will be great among you, let him be your minister..." We get an even better picture of His message to his disciples in Mark 10:42-45(KJV), "But Jesus called them to him, and saith unto them, Ye know that they which are accounted to rule over the Gentiles exercise lordship over them; and their great ones exercise authority upon them. But so shall it not be among you: but whosoever will be great among you, shall be your minister: And whosoever of you will be the chiefest, shall be servant of all. For even the Son of man came, not to be ministered unto, but to minister and to give his life a ransom for many."

From these passages, we get a clearer understanding of what it means to be a minister. The whole point of being a minister is to serve others. Jesus said that this is the way you can become great in the Kingdom of God. If you want to be chief among those with whom you serve, then don't let them out do you in serving others. One of the things I have always appreciated about my home church, Faith Christian Center in Jacksonville, Florida, is our attitude and disposition toward serving others in excellence. In fact, at my church you could get run over by someone leaping at an opportunity to serve. Why do we respond to serving with such delight? It is because we have been taught that the key to growing spiritually and going to the next level is in serving others. But more importantly, it is the most Christ-like thing we can do as believers.

Loyalty and Commitment

The Lord will always test your loyalty and commitment to those he places over you. Just as Elijah did not force Elisha to follow him, Jesus will not force you to follow Him. You will be following Jesus when you follow the man or woman He places over you. Elisha was never forced at any time to follow Elijah. When Elijah met him initially, he told him that he had a choice to stay and work in his field, or to follow him. Elisha chose to follow Elijah because he knew that it was God, not Elijah, who was calling him into the ministry. Yet, we see Elisha followed and submitted to Elijah's leadership. He became Elijah's assistant, the one who ran his errands, the one who gave him water to drink.

Like Elisha, you must also know that it is God, not man, who has called you in to the ministry. When you are there up-close with the man or woman of God, an impartation takes place. This impartation is caught, not learned. This impartation is the anointing for you to carry out the same or a similar ministry when it is time for your promotion.

2 *Kings* 2:9, 10

9 *And so it was, when they had crossed over, that Elijah said to Elisha, "Ask! What may I do for you, before I am taken away from you?"*

Elisha said, "Please let a double portion of your spirit be upon me."

10 *So he said, "You have asked a hard thing; Nevertheless, if you see me when I am taken from you, it shall be so for you; but if not, it shall not be so"*

So often we want the benefits of ministry without the sacrifices of ministry. Elisha asked Elijah for a double portion of his spirit before he left. He had been there and watched Elijah prophesy, he watched him raise the dead, he knew that Elijah stopped the rain for three and a half years, and he knew that there was a great anointing on Elijah. Elisha had come to the place where he really wanted what Elijah had. It is a great testimony when someone who follows you wants to be just like you. It says that you must have been doing things God's way. It speaks of your commitment and loyalty to God. It speaks of your walk of faith and integrity. These are the attributes of godly leadership. Godly leadership is always attractive because the anointing of God rests upon it. The anointing of God is always attractive to others.

2 *Kings* 2:11, 12

11 *Then it happened, as they continued on and talked, that suddenly a chariot of fire appeared with horses of fire, and separated the two of them; and Elijah went up by a whirlwind into heaven.*

12 *And Elisha saw it, and he cried out, "My father, my father, the chariot of Israel and its horsemen!" So he saw him no more. And he took hold of his own clothes and tore them into two pieces.*

So, Elijah said to Elisha, "If you see me when I am taken

away, you can have a double portion of my anointing." What a challenge! He was saying to Elisha, it is yours if you stay faithful; it is yours if you stay committed; it is yours if you keep serving with your whole heart; it is yours if you stay with me until the very end.

That is still the message to ministers today. You can have a double portion of God's anointing if you stay committed, loyal and faithful until the very end. The very end is your beginning. The very end is your promotion. Though you may have served for years, your promotion can come in one day and your life will be changed forever. It is recorded that Elijah performed sixteen miracles in his ministry, but Elisha performed thirty-two miracles in his. He did indeed receive a double portion of Elijah's anointing. Elisha was there to catch his mantle when it fell from the sky on the day he was taken away to heaven.

Mantle Ministry

Ministering under the covering of another
Follow-ship that leads to Leader-ship

THE PURPOSE OF MANTLE MINISTRY

According to Malachi 4, before the day of the coming of the Lord, He will send Elijah to turn the heart of the fathers to the children and the heart of the children to their fathers. Matthew 11:7-14 reveals that this prophecy refers to John the Baptist who came in the spirit and power of Elijah – Luke 1:17. While this passage of scripture may refer to a natural father and children relationship, its primary reference is to a spiritual father and son relationship. Elijah was a spiritual father to the nation of Israel as well as Elisha and John the Baptist. Their assignment was to turn the hearts of the people back to God. We saw this take place on Mount Carmel, where Elijah said to the nation "How long will you be caught between two opinions? If the Lord be God, follow Him: but if Baal, then follow him." – 1 Kings 18:21. We also see it in Matthew 3 where John called the nation of Israel to repentance and said that the Kingdom of God is at hand.

Therefore, the spirit of Elijah is about reviving the family of God and bring it back to God. Here we get the essence of the father's ministry. His role is to bring the children (the sons and daughters) back to God. We also see this essence in the relationship between Elijah and Elisha. Elijah prepared Elisha to father the nation of Israel in his absence. The father-son relationship is all about perpetuating the Kingdom of God from generation to generation. The Elijah-Elisha relationship is a good example of a spiritual father and son relationship for the expressed purpose of furthering the Kingdom of God.

I believe that in the culminating days of this world, we are going to see a prolific expression of the ministry of Elijah in the Body of Christ, the Bride of Christ, as she prepares herself to join Him when He returns. My intent for Mantle Ministry is to remind us of the importance of developing the father-son relationships in ministry and to help ministers, on a larger scale, prepare themselves, as well as the Bride, for the second coming of our Lord Jesus Christ. My main purpose for writing Mantle Ministry is to provide yet another means to augment the prophetic promise of "turning the heart of leaders to the followers and heart of the followers to the leaders". Not just to bring it to the fore front of our thinking, but to provide a model plan for carrying it out as well.

The concept of Mantle Ministry was taken from the life and times of Elijah and Elisha as recorded in 2 Kings 2:1-15. As mentioned earlier, there are four stages in Mantle Ministry. In each stage, Elijah serves as a good example of a leader and Elisha is a good example of a follower who eventually leads. By examining the Elijah-Elisha relationship, we see the father-son relationship at work. Now let's take a closer look at the four stages of Mantle Ministry.

2 *Kings* 2:1-6

1 *And it came to pass, when the* LORD *would take up Elijah into* *heaven by a whirlwind, that Elijah went with Elisha from Gilgal.*

2 And Elijah said unto Elisha, Tarry here, I pray thee; for the LORD hath sent me to Bethel. And Elisha said unto him, As the LORD liveth, and as thy soul liveth, I will not leave thee. So they went down to Bethel.

3 And the sons of the prophets that were at Bethel came forth to Elisha, and said unto him, Knowest thou that the LORD will take away thy master from thy head today? And he said, Yea, I know it; hold ye your peace.

4 And Elijah said unto him, Elisha, tarry here, I pray thee; for the LORD hath sent me to Jericho. And he said, As the LORD liveth, and as thy soul liveth, I will not leave thee. So they came to Jericho.

5 And the sons of the prophets that were at Jericho came to Elisha, and said unto him, Knowest thou that the LORD will take away thy master from thy head today? And he answered, Yea, I know it; hold ye your peace.

6 And Elijah said unto him, Tarry, I pray thee, here; for the LORD hath sent me to Jordan. And he said, As the LORD liveth, and as thy soul liveth, I will not leave thee. And they two went on.

Acts 1:8

8 But ye shall receive power, after that the Holy Ghost is come upon you: and ye shall be witnesses unto me both in Jerusalem, and in all Judaea, and in Samaria, and unto the uttermost part of the earth.

Notice how consistent the word of God is. We see four stages of ministry in 2 Kings 2:1-6, Gilgal, Bethel, Jericho and Jordan. We also see four stages of ministry in Acts 1:8, Jerusalem, Judaea, Samaria and the Uttermost Parts. God tells us what do in Acts 1:8 and He shows us how to do it in 2 Kings 2:1-6, 7-15. I have always gone to the Old Testament to get examples of what I am told to do in the New Testament.

In this chapter I want to emphasize the importance of the experience gained from going through each of the four stages of mantle ministry. Just as it was for Elisha, your challenge will be to stick with your Elijah during the tough times, the rough times, and the mundane times. It is crucial that you keep up with your Elijah. Don't let him get away from you. You have to be where he is so that you don't miss anything that God does through him. You never know what month, week, day or hour that God will work a miracle through your Elijah. But most importantly, you want to be there when your Elijah gets his promotion so that you can catch his mantle. Now let's take a closer look at the mantle.

THE MANTLE OF ANOTHER

2 Kings 2:13-15

13 *He also took up the mantle of Elijah that had fallen from him, and went back and stood by the bank of the Jordan.*

14 *Then he took the mantle of Elijah that had fallen from him, and struck the water, and said, "Where is the LORD God of Elijah?" And when he also had struck the water, it was divided this way and that; and Elisha crossed over.*

15 *Now when the sons of the prophets who were from Jericho saw him, they said, "The spirit of Elijah rests on Elisha." And they came to meet him, and bowed to the ground before him*

Observe that the anointed mantle of Elijah was the very thing that got Elisha over. There was a residue of Elijah's anointing in that mantle. In fact, there was a double portion of his anointing in that mantle. You will be able to teach and preach just as your leadership does. You will be able to lead others just as your leadership led you.

Now that you know that your anointing is in the mantle of your leadership; you will be able to immediately draw from that anointing when the mantle falls on you. The mantle will fall on you on the day of your promotion. God will make it happen to you. He knows when you are ready for it. Your leadership will also know when you are ready for it as well. God will cause you to be promoted on a day when you least expect it. It will be the day when the mantle of your leadership falls on you.

In the meantime, you should maintain the same attitude and disposition that Elisha had. Don't listen to those around you who are telling you that you should be out front leading because of your anointed skills and abilities. Don't let them push you out before your time. Just as Elijah and Elisha knew when it was Elisha's time to catch the falling mantle, you will know when it's your time to catch the falling mantle of your leadership. Remember, "God is not a man that He should lie; neither the son of man that He should repent; has He spoken and shall he not make it good?" – Numbers 23:19. "Be of good courage and wait on the Lord. For the vision is yet for an appointed time, but at the end it shall speak, and not lie: though it tarry, wait for it: because it will surely come, it will not tarry "- Habakkuk 2:3.

THE PURPOSE OF THE MANTLE

To get a better understanding of the concept of Mantle Ministry, we must first understand the purpose and use of the mantle that the man of God wore. The Mantle was a distinctive Hebrew outer garment made of two pieces of thick woolen material sewn together, with slits rather than sleeves for the arms. In Old Testament times the mantle was usually brightly colored. Joseph's "tunic of many colors" was probably a mantle of woven, bright strips – Genesis 37:3. The Lord commanded the people of Israel to add blue tassels to the corners of their outer garments, or their mantles, to remind them to obey His commandments - Numbers 15:38. In a similar way, Mantle Ministry is designed to helps young ministers find their true purpose which is to fulfill God's greater purpose for mankind.

A COVERING

The mantle was a covering for sleep and comfort - John 14:16, 26. The typical Hebrew slept on the floor with his mantle as a covering to keep him warm. This was especially true for travelers, shepherds, or poor people. A person's mantle was not to be kept as collateral for a loan -Exodus 22:26. In times of anguish, the Hebrews often tore their mantles to show their distress - Job 2:12; Ezra 9:3.

A handy, one-piece garment, the mantle protected a person from the weather. Because it fitted loosely, it could also be used to conceal or carry items. The typical Jewish mantle hung below the knees and was decorated with fringes. Other words for the mantle used by various English translations are cloak, coat, robe, and wimple. (Nelson's Illustrated Bible Dictionary)(Copyright (C) 1986, Thomas Nelson Publishers)

The mantle was a square piece of material like a blanket or plaid. In pleasant weather it was more conveniently worn over the shoulders than wrapped around the body. Although it answered the purpose of a cloak, it was also large enough to carry food and personal belongings in it - Exodus. 12:34; 2 Kings 4:39. The poor wrapped themselves up wholly in this garment at night. They would spread their leather girdle upon a rock and rest the head upon it, as is customary to this day in Asia. Moses, therefore, enacted a law of what had been a custom, that the upper garment, when given as a pledge, should not be retained

21

overnight - Exodus 22:26 27; Deuteronomy 24:13; Job 22:6; 24:7. In the time of Christ, creditors did not take the upper garment or cloak because it was not lawful for them to retain - Matthew 5:40.

It is from this backdrop of information about the use of the Old Testament mantle that we extract the concept of mantle ministry. Thus, mantle ministry is a covering for young followers as they develop into mature ministers. Furthermore, we see why it is so vital for every young follower to be under the covering of a senior minister as in the case of Elisha with Elijah.

THE FRINGE BENEFIT

Numbers 15:37-40

37 And the LORD spake unto Moses, saying,

38 Speak unto the children of Israel, and bid them that they make them fringes in the borders of their garments throughout their generations, and that they put upon the fringe of the borders a ribbon of blue:

39 And it shall be unto you for a fringe, that ye may look upon it, and remember all the commandments of the LORD, and do them; and that ye seek not after your own heart and your own eyes, after which ye use to go a whoring:

40 That ye may remember, and do all my commandments, and be holy unto your God.

We get the concept of fringe benefit from this passage of scripture. The same concept of the fringe benefit is used today at the workplace. An employer tells a prospective employee that if he or she comes to work for them they will receive the company's fringe benefits of a paid vacation, matching funds in their 401K and medical insurance.

Did you know that you too have fringe benefits in the kingdom of God? Let me lay them out for you. All your iniquities are forgiven. You are healed of all your diseases. Your life is redeemed from destruction. You have been crowned with loving-kindness and tender mercies. You mouth is satisfied with good things and your youth is renewed like the eagle's – Psalm 103:2-5. All these fringe benefits come with the robe of righteousness (mantle) you received when you said yes to Jesus Christ.

The fringe benefit of healing was what the women with the issue of blood got from Jesus. She said if I could just touch the hem of his garment (mantle) I will be made whole. Notice, she did not say well. She said whole. Did you know that you could possibly get healed of a disease and it could come back, but if you are made whole, the sickness is completely eradicated, gone for good. This word whole also carries the idea that one is made whole in every aspect of his or her life – Mark 5:25-34.

In Matthew 15:21-28, the Canaanite Woman also wanted some of the fringe benefit (healing for her daughter). Jesus called it the children's bread. Here you have the concept of bread or food taken from the mantle. But, this woman was determined to get this healing bread for her daughter. Even after Jesus told her that the healing she sought was for the children of Abraham and should not be given to dogs; she said, "Yes Lord but even the dogs eat the crumbs that fall from their masters' table." Jesus then said, "O women, great is thy faith: be it unto you even as you will."

Notice that Jesus said even as you will. Why did Jesus change his mind and let her have the fringe benefit that was only for the children of Abraham? He had no choice, because the woman that He called a dog had become a daughter of Abraham. In this very instance, she exercised the faith of Abraham and it was accounted to her as right-standing with God – Galatians 3:6-9.

I once preached a message on this passage of scripture titled "the dog that became a daughter". You see the woman got into faith that pleased God. And he that comes to Him must believe that He is and that He rewards those who diligently seek Him – Hebrews 11:1, 2, 6.

Now here are some scriptural references to the mantle, cloak or garment. In the New Testament it is often referred to as a robe of righteousness, which the believer receives at conversion:

Matthew 9:20

And, behold, a woman, which was diseased with an issue of blood twelve years, came behind him, and touched the hem of his garment.

Acts 19:11-12

And God wrought special miracles by the hands of Paul: So that from his body were brought unto the sick handkerchiefs or aprons, and the diseases departed from them, and the evil spirits went out of them.

Isaiah 61:10

I will greatly rejoice in the LORD, my soul shall be joyful in my God; for He hath clothed me with the garments of salvation, He hath covered me with the robe of righteousness, as a bridegroom decketh himself with ornaments, and as a bride adorneth herself with her jewels.

Revelation 7:9

After this I beheld, and, lo, a great multitude, which no man could number, of all nations, and kindreds, and people, and tongues, stood before the throne, and before the Lamb, clothed with white robes, and palms in their hands.

Revelation 7:14

And I said unto him, Sir, thou knowest. And he said to me, These are they which came out of great tribulation, and have washed their robes, and made them white in the blood of the Lamb.

In Chapter 3, I go into more detail about this, but we as believers have the mantle of Jesus. Ephesians 1:3 says that we have been blessed with all spiritual blessing in heavenly places in Christ. According to Romans 8:17 we are joint heirs with Christ, and John 15:16 says that Jesus has given us the authority of His name on the earth. From this we can see that the mantle represents the presence of the one it belongs to, or the one who gives it. What a mighty God we serve!

Eating from the Right Pot

2 Kings 4:38-41
38 *And Elisha came again to Gilgal: and there was a dearth in the land; and the sons of the prophets were sitting before him: and he said unto his servant, Set on the great pot, and seethe pottage for the sons of the prophets.*

39 *And one went out into the field to gather herbs, and found a wild vine, and gathered thereof wild gourds, his lap full, and came and shred them into the pot of pottage: for they knew them not.*

40 *So they poured out for the men to eat. And it came to pass, as they were eating of the pottage, that they cried out, and said, O thou man of God, there is death in the pot. And they could not eat thereof.*

41 *He said bring meal. And he cast it into the pot; and he said, Pour out for the people, that they may eat. And there was no harm in the pot.*

The mantle was used by the Old Testament Prophets to gather and store food. In the case of the Sons of the Prophets, they were feed poisonous food by a careless gatherer who went out in to the field and gathered wild herbs into his mantle and put them in the pot. We should always be careful about whose mantle we eat from. This should be a reminder to us that we can't eat from everyone. The purpose of your pastor or shepherd is to lead you to food that is sufficient for you. All of the good pastors that I've had over the years would never let just anyone come into their pulpit to feed us. The ones they would allow to feed us were always a blessing and we never had a stomach ache after eating.

Just because someone is a Christian, is not necessarily advisable to eat from his or her mantle. As in the case of the Prophets who were following Elisha, while they were students of his, they ate from another's mantle and it was poisonous to them. Why? Because that leader was careless with the way he prepared the food for them. Many times it's not that the person does not have a legitimate relationship with Jesus Christ, but rather, he or she just may not be called to feed you. You may not be called to the purpose God has called him or her to, and they may not be called to the purpose God has called you to. But if you are under God-given leadership, that leadership will always feed you with healthy nutritious food that will cause you to grow in ministry and prepare you to fulfill the purpose God has called you to.

Ultimately, Mantle Ministry should serve to help young followers find their true purpose and to know that their purpose is to fulfill God's greater purpose for mankind. It is from this context that we understand the importance of a young follower staying under the cover of a more mature leader. This relationship affords the young follower the opportunity to grow in the things of God by seeing and experiencing, first-hand, God working in and through the more mature leader. This relationship will serve to ground the young follower in the love of God, in biblical doctrine, in Christian character and integrity, and in humility. These godly attributes are essential for a successful ministry to be sustained throughout the life of the young follower.

Chapter 3

The Mantle of Jesus

Ministering under the covering of another
Follow-ship that leads to Leader-ship

I believe that the mantle of Elijah is a type of Holy Spirit as the Mantle of Jesus. Jesus always operated under the covering of His Father - the Father's Holy Spirit. I have compiled the following Old and New Testament scriptures to support this premise. Let's take a careful look at the following scriptures to see, if indeed, the mantle is a type of Holy Spirit:

2 Kings 2:11-14
11 *And it came to pass, as they still went on, and talked, that, behold, there appeared a chariot of fire, and horses of fire, and parted them both asunder; and Elijah went up by a whirlwind into heaven.*
12 *And Elisha saw it, and he cried, my father, my father, the chariot of Israel, and the horsemen thereof. And he saw him no more: and he took hold of his own clothes, and rent them in two pieces.*
13 *He took up also the mantle of Elijah that fell from him, and went back, and stood by the bank of Jordan;*
14 *And he took the mantle of Elijah that fell from him, and smote the waters, and said, Where is the LORD God of Elijah? and when he also had smitten the waters, they parted hither and thither: and Elisha went over.*

Leviticus 23:15-16

And ye shall count unto you from the morrow after the sabbath, from the day that ye brought the sheaf of the wave offering; seven sabbaths shall be complete: Even unto the morrow after the seventh sabbath shall ye number fifty days; and ye shall offer a new meat offering unto the LORD.

John 14:16, 26

16 *And I will pray the Father, and he shall give you another Comforter, that he may abide with you forever;....*

26 *But the Comforter, which is the Holy Ghost, whom the Father will send in my name, he shall teach you all things, and bring all things to your remembrance, whatsoever I have said unto you.*

John 15:26-27

But when the Comforter is come, whom I will send unto you from the Father, even the Spirit of truth, which proceedeth from the Father, he shall testify of me: And ye also shall bear witness, because ye have been with me from the beginning.

John 16:7

Nevertheless I tell you the truth; It is expedient for you that I go away: for if I go not away, the Comforter will not come unto you; but if I depart, I will send him unto you.

John 20:22

And when he had said this, he breathed on them, and saith unto them, Receive ye the Holy Ghost.

Acts 1:4-5

And, being assembled together with them, commanded them that they should not depart from Jerusalem, but wait for the promise of the Father, which, saith he, ye have heard of me. For John truly baptized with water; but ye shall be baptized with the Holy Ghost not many days hence.

Acts 2:1-4

1 And *when the day of Pentecost was fully come, they were all with one accord in one place.*

2 And *suddenly there came a sound from heaven as of a rushing mighty wind, and it filled all the house where they were sitting.*

3 And *there appeared unto them cloven tongues like as of fire, and it sat upon each of them.*

4 And *they were all filled with the Holy Ghost, and began to speak with other tongues, as the Spirit gave them utterance.*

Holy Spirit was given as a promise gift from Father God, sent to the believer by His Son Jesus, who is the first-fruit of the harvest. Jesus sent Holy Spirit seven Sabbaths (50 days) after he returned to heaven. The Day of Pentecost in Acts 2 was a fulfillment of Leviticus 23:15-16. 2 Kings 2:11-14 is a depiction of Holy Spirit, which was to fall on the Day of Pentecost and on all believers thereafter.

ATTRIBUTES OF THE MANTLE

Furthermore, the mantle of the Old Testament carries the attributes of Holy Spirit. It was a covering and comfort, so is Holy Spirit today in the life of the believer. It was used for protection from the harsh elements. Today Holy Spirit warns and guides the believer away from danger or hash elements. The mantle was used to gather and store food. Holy Spirit feeds the believer by imparting wisdom, knowledge and understanding, and by reminding the believer of the Word that is stored up in his or her own spirit. Just as the Mantle fell from Elijah when he went up to heaven, Holy Spirit fell from Jesus when he went up to heaven.

MANTLE OF THE HIGH PRIEST

One day while living in Iceland, Holy Spirit gave me a revelation of Jesus dressed in His Priestly garments like the Priest in the Old Testament. The Old Testament Priest wore a gorgeous robe with tassels, bells, and pomegranates at the hem. The High Priest was required to take the blood of a lamb into the Holy of Holies once a year to atone for the sins of the nation of Israel. If the High Priest had sin in his own life, he would die before God while in the Holy of Holies – Leviticus 16.

As you can imagine, the Priest took this duty very seriously and the Israelites would be concerned about his welfare while he ministered in the Holy of Holies. Tradition has it, that when the Priest would move around in the Holy of Holies, the Israelites could hear him because the bells tinkled when they came in contact with the tassels and pomegranates on the hem of his robe (mantle). This sound let the Israelites know that the Priest was still alive and well in the Holy of Holies. This is the same picture that Holy Spirit showed me of Jesus in his present day ministry in heaven. Scripture tells us that New Testament believers are the Body of Christ. Just as the bells would tinkle when the earthly Priest would minister in the Holy of Holies, we too tinkle as members of the Body of Christ as He ministers in the heavenly sanctuary today. This tinkling is done when we speak in other tongues. Our tongues are an indication to the world that Jesus is alive and well in the heavenly sanctuary - Glory be to God forever!

The revelation I received from studying these passages of scriptures is that Holy Spirit is the Mantle of Jesus. Therefore, it is crucial that you know the importance of receiving the baptism of Holy Spirit, if you haven't already. The baptism of Holy Spirit is not necessary to be saved, but He is necessary to walk in the miraculous power and anointing of God. Interestingly, Holy Spirit came upon Elijah and Elisha as well as other Old Testament prophets, and yet He still comes upon the believer today. Acts 1:13 and 2:3-4 say that, when **Holy Spirit came upon on those in the upper room on the day of Pentecost, they were filled with Holy Spirit and spoke in tongues**. Notice that Holy Spirit came upon them, then they were filled with Him and then they spoke in tongues. This is the pattern of how Holy Spirit baptizes the believer throughout the Book of Acts.

BAPTISM AS A SIGN

What we should remember is that the born-again experience is unique to the New Testament believer and it speaks of the inward work of Holy Spirit within the believer – John 3:3-6. The Greek word for Baptism is Baptizo. It means to immerse, overflow or drench. Thus, when the Mantle of Jesus comes upon you, He immerses you, drenches you and overflows upon you. The overflow comes when you are filled, just as you would continue to pour water into a cup until it overflows. When this distinctive characteristic of Holy Spirit overflows upon you, you will begin to speak in tongues as He gives you utterance. This is evident by what took place on the Day of Pentecost and in subsequent events in the book of the Acts. When believers were baptized in Holy Spirit, others could hear and see it. Hearing the tongues and seeing the change in the countenance of the believer is the distinct indication that the baptism of Holy Spirit has taken place.

The Born-Again experience, for the most part, can take place in a quiet manner unnoticed by others. By all Biblical standards, no one can judge whether or not someone has been born again. But, anyone can hear and see when someone is or has been baptized in Holy Spirit. I believe God has fashioned the baptism of Holy Spirit this way because He meant for it to be something that could be heard and seen. Because we have so many people out there making an intellectual argument against the new birth experience, as we progress towards the closing days of the world, I believe we are going to see more and more of the hearing and seeing aspects of the baptism of Holy Spirit as a clear distinction between those who are truly born again and those who are not.

Furthermore, you need the Baptism of Holy Spirit to receive a greater understanding of the word of God. You need Him to receive revelations form God. You need Him to preach and teach God's Word, with boldness and power, under the anointed presence of Holy Spirit. Have you ever noticed that believers who are not baptized in Holy Spirit also do not claim any of the miraculous power of Holy Spirit in their lives? They do not grasp a deeper understanding of God and the things of God. They tend to deal with God in an impersonal way. Those who are baptized in Holy Spirit openly speak of their intimate relationship with God, Jesus and Holy Spirit in a personal and endearing way. On the other hand, those who are not baptized in Holy Spirit, talk about God but not to Him. They tend to have a hard time believing that God would speak directly to someone in a personal way. For instance, a Spirit-filled believer might say that "God spoke to me this morning". Whereas a believer who is not baptized in Holy Spirit would probably say, "I spent time in devotion this morning and I am impressed to do this or that today."

Obviously, one can go overboard with or without the baptism of Holy Spirit. We have ample examples of both extremes. But, this does not diminish the fact that a believer baptized in Holy Spirit tends to relate to God, Jesus, and Holy Spirit in a more personal way, and in a more intimate way as well. They tend to use intimate language to describe their relationship with God. This simply conforms to the intimate relationship the believer is to have with God, Jesus and Holy Spirit as found in John 14 and 15. There is ample scripture instructing the believer to actively seek an intimate relationship with God through His Son Jesus Christ, by the agency of His Holy Spirit. In fact, Jesus says in John 14:23, that He and the Father, through Holy Spirit, would (make their abode) live within the believer.

Leadership
and Followship

Ministering under the covering of another
Follow-ship that leads to Leader-ship

There is a follow-ship that leads to leader-ship. Leader-ship and follow-ship are like a father and son relationship. In scripture Paul addresses Timothy as his spiritual son – 1 Timothy 1:2 and 2 Timothy 1:2. When we study their relationship we can see that Timothy became a great leader. He became the pastor of one of the largest churches in Asia Minor, and ultimately attained the position of bishop; one who has oversight over other churches. His growth and development was a direct result of his fellowship with Paul as well as following the guidance and counsel given to him by Paul. In Philippians 2:20, Paul says that he did not have any one else who had his mind like Timothy did. They were likeminded because of their father-son relationship. The father-son relationship is a work of Holy Spirit in the father and the son. Holy Spirit causes them to work together in unity and same-mindedness to accomplish God's purpose for their lives.

35

Furthermore, fellowship is the key ingredient that causes the follower to grow to be a leader. Jesus had twelve followers who fellowshipped with Him. As they fellowshipped with Him they were able to observe him in action and to hear what he said and to see what he did. They were close enough to actually catch the vision rather than theorizing about it. This is like the father and son situation where the very attributes of the father are imparted to the son. That is what took place in the Elijah-Elisha relationship. This is that precious relationship you want to have with your Elijah. Don't settle for less. Ask God to lead you to your Elijah. You will know him when you find him because he has been looking for you. The Lord has already told him to take you under his wings and teach you all that he knows. So, go ahead and put yourself under his authority and leadership, and you will grow up to be a great minister just as Elisha did.

No Lone-Rangers in the Kingdom

I Kings 19:14-17

14 *And he said, I have been very jealous for the LORD God of hosts: because the children of Israel have forsaken thy covenant, thrown down thine altars, and slain thy prophets with the sword; and I, even I only, am left; and they seek my life, to take it away.*

15 *And the LORD said unto him, Go, return on thy way to the wilderness of Damascus: and when thou comest, anoint Hazael to be king over Syria:*

16 *And Jehu the son of Nimshi shalt thou anoint to be king over Israel: and Elisha the son of Shaphat of Abelmeholah shalt thou anoint to be prophet in thy room.*

17 *And it shall come to pass, that him that escapeth the sword of Hazael shall Jehu slay: and him that escapeth from the sword of Jehu shall Elisha slay.*

God wanted Elijah to know that He does not work alone and neither should he. Our principle application from this passage is that a leader should not work alone but should groom God-chosen followers to help with the ministry. It is called the Ministry of Helps in the New Testament.

1 Corinthians 12:28 says "And God hath set some in the Church, first apostles, secondarily prophets, thirdly teachers, after that miracles, the gifts of healings, helps, governments, diversities of tongues." In the mist of these offices that God has set in the church, we see the Ministry of Helps (MOH) right in the middle of them all. This is a good indicator to us that God sees the Ministry of Helps as being very important to the orderly function of the church. Now let's take a look at another passage of scripture that deals with the Ministry of Helps in the Old Testament.

MINISTERING TO YOUR LEADER

Numbers 11:14-17

14 *I am not able to bear all this people alone, because it is too heavy for me.*

15 *And if thou deal thus with me, kill me, I pray thee, out of hand, if I have found favour in thy sight; and let me not see my wretchedness.*

16 *And the LORD said unto Moses, Gather unto me seventy men of the elders of Israel, whom thou knowest to be the elders of the people, and officers over them; and bring them unto the tabernacle of the congregation, that they may stand there with thee.*

17 *And I will come down and talk with thee there: and I will take of the spirit which is upon thee, and will put it upon them; and they shall bear the burden of the people with thee, that thou bear it not thyself alone.*

In this passage we see God instructing Moses to choose seventy men to help lead and minister to the Israelites. God also told Moses that He would take of his spirit and put it on those he had chosen to follow him. Like those Moses chose to follow him, and God placing his spirit on them; God will also take of your Elijah's spirit and place it on you. Once you come under his leadership and began ministering to him by assisting him with the ministry, you will begin to discern his spirit upon you. The more you stay around him, the more you will act like him, talk like him and even walk like him. This is the work of God in your life to ultimately make you a spiritual son of your Elijah.

Therefore, followers should minister to their leader because ministering to your leader is ministering to God. This is supported by Old and New Testament scriptures. It is a work of grace that puts you in a humble position for God to exalt you in due season. But when you are exalted, you should continue to minister in humility throughout the course of your ministry.

A Servant's Heart

Isaiah 48:17

Thus saith the LORD, thy Redeemer, the Holy One of Israel; I am the LORD thy God which teacheth thee to profit, which leadeth thee by the way that thou shouldest go.

1 Timothy 3:13

For they that have used the office of a deacon well purchase to themselves a good degree, and great boldness in the faith which is in Christ Jesus.

Isaiah 48:17 says that God teaches His people how to profit as He leads them in the way they should go. Although 1Timothy

3:13 is dealing with the office of a deacon, we know by definition of the word deacon, we get one who serves others. From this verse of scripture we can deduce that the emphasis is on providing service to others. This verse also says that those who serve others purchase for themselves a good degree, and great boldness in the faith which is in Christ Jesus. We can also conclude from this verse that those who serve will excel in the things of God, grow more readily into maturity and become bolder in their faith.

We see this very thing in the life of Stephen in Acts chapters 6 and 7, and similarly in the case of Phillip in Acts 8:5-13. The scriptures say that Stephen was full of the Holy Spirit and had great boldness in his presentation of the Gospel. Here you have a deacon, a servant, who gains a powerful mastery of God's entire redemptive plan for the salvation of mankind by waiting on tables. Even though Stephen was not an apostle, no apostle had a better grasp of the kingdom of God than Stephen. In Acts chapter 7, Stephen gives one of the most remarkable accounts of God's redemptive plan for man, from the time of Abraham to his present day. His account was so brilliantly done that it caused Jesus to get up out of His seat in Heaven and hail him. Like Stephen, you too can purchase for yourself a good degree in Jesus and have great boldness in your faith by serving your leader and others. In my walk with God over the years, I have observed that those who serve others mature quicker and have a better handle on their place in the Kingdom.

What we must remember is that the Kingdom of God does not operate like the world. In the world you compete to get ahead and try to out-do others. In the Kingdom of God, you serve others to get a head. In the world you get to gain. In the Kingdom of God you lose to gain, and give to receive. By giving your service away you will gain in growth, maturity, boldness in your faith and be pleasing to God as well.

The ultimate example of a servant is Jesus Christ as recorded in Philippians 2:5-11. This passage of scripture says that we should have the same mind that Christ has when it comes to serving. Even though He was God, He did not seek a reputation for himself, but took upon Himself a servant's status. He humbled himself to serve others and was obedient in service, even obedient enough to die in service for all of mankind. Because of his service, God has highly exalted Him and given Him a name that is above every name: that at the name of Jesus every knee shall bow, of things in heaven, and things in earth, and things under the earth; and that every tongue should confess that Jesus Christ is Lord, to the glory of God the Father. This is one of my favorite passages of scripture because it so adequately shows our profit from our service to others. God promoted Jesus because of His **service, obedience** and *humility*. These are three attributes of a servant's heart that will sustain you as a minister and cause you to be successful in ministry.

The New Testament believer no longer has the status of a servant but should live the Christian life with a servant's heart – John 15:15.

THE INSIDE SCOOP

In John Chapter 2 we have the account of Jesus turning water into wine. Mary the mother of Jesus came to Him and tells Him that there is no more wine for the guests at the wedding. Jesus replies with - it's not time for me to minister yet. Then Mary tells the servants, "Whatever He says, do it." Jesus tells the servant to fill six pots with water and then the water is turned into wine.

First of all, Jesus always did what the Father told him to

do. So when Mary made her request, evidently Jesus had not heard the Father say that. But Mary's request and her faith must have moved the Father to change the time for Jesus to begin His ministry. So, Jesus heard the change in instructions from the Father, and proceeded to perform his first miracle. I believe God responded to two things in this little scenario - Mary's faith and her desire to serve others. Let me say this again - because of Mary's faith and her desire to serve others, God fast-forwarded the time for Jesus' first miracle.

What I also observed in this account was the position of the servants. They were in a position to see Jesus; to hear Jesus, to join Jesus in the making of the miracle; and to observe what He did. This wine was so good that the governor at the wedding asked the bridegroom, "Where did he get it from?" He said, "It's better than the first glass I had. Most folks would have served the good stuff first and left the worse for last. But you have saved the best for last. Notice that God always saves the best for last and the last becomes the first." He never changes. When you experience what he does, it is the best at that moment.

My main point here is that the servants were in position to get the inside scoop on the making of a miracle. They were able to participate in the making of the miracle. They also had a front row seat to observe the miracle-making process. You too, will be in a position to get the inside scoop on what Jesus is doing in His Kingdom when you are in a position of serving others. Your service to others will put you in the place to see Jesus working. You will be able to hear when He tells you to do something. You will be able to join Him in His work and to observe all the details of how miracles are performed. This will be invaluable training for you and it will boost your faith in God. But more importantly, you will be in a position to work miracles with Jesus. What a reward for your service!

Therefore, by virtue of position, a servant gets the inside scoop on the inner workings of the Kingdom of God. These are some things to remember about the profits of a servant's heart:

1. The greatest attribute of a servant is Humility - Micah 6:8, Philippians 2:8.

2. Your service should be a work of faith – James 2:14-26.

3. God provides for providers - I Kings 3:4-15.

4. God reveals his secrets to those with a servant's heart – Amos 3:7 vs. John 2:5-9.

The Gilgal Ministry

Ministering under the covering of another
Follow-ship that leads to Leader-ship

STAGE ONE

Followers should begin at Gilgal. Gilgal is the First Stage of Mantel Ministry. It is the place of new beginnings.

2 Kings 2:1
And it came to pass, when the LORD would take up Elijah into heaven by a whirlwind, that Elijah went with Elisha from Gilgal.

Joshua 5:2-9
2 At that time the LORD said unto Joshua, Make thee sharp knives, and circumcise again the children of Israel the second time.

3 And Joshua made him sharp knives, and circumcised the children of Israel at the hill of the foreskins.

4 And this is the cause why Joshua did circumcise: All the people that came out of Egypt, that were males, even all the men of war, died in the wilderness by the way, after they came out of Egypt.

5 Now all the people that came out were circumcised: but all the people that were born in the wilderness by the way as they came forth out of Egypt, *them they had not circumcised.*

6 *For the children of Israel walked forty years in the wilderness, till all the people that were men of war, which came out of Egypt, were consumed, because they obeyed not the voice of the LORD: unto whom the LORD sware that he would not shew them the land, which the LORD sware unto their fathers that he would give us, a land that floweth with milk and honey.*

7 *And their children, whom he raised up in their stead, them Joshua circumcised: for they were uncircumcised, because they had not circumcised them by the way.*

8 *And it came to pass, when they had done circumcising all the people, that they abode in their places in the camp, till they were whole.*

9 *And the LORD said unto Joshua, This day have I rolled away the reproach of Egypt from off you. Wherefore the name of the place is called Gilgal unto this day.*

THE PLACE OF NEW-BEGINNINGS

Gilgal is the First Stage of Mantle Ministry. Gilgal is known as the Place of Cutting, the place of new-birth and new-beginnings. It was at Gilgal that God directed Joshua to circumcise (to cut the foreskin of every male child) the new generation of Israelites who were born in the wilderness. They are often referred to as the Joshua-Generation. In circumcising this new generation, Joshua carried out the commandment God had given Abraham – Genesis 17:12-13.

Notice that this cutting or circumcision was done with a knife or a sword. Thus, we get the concept of the cutting-sword or a "Cutting-Word." Sword is a type of the Word of God in scripture. Interestingly, the word sword is nothing more than "WORD" proceeded by an "S", which forms the word (S/WORD). This is a clever way of showing how the Word of God functions like a sword.

Swords are used in cutting flesh. It was the instrument used to perform circumcision on all the 8-day old male Israelite babies. Likewise, the New Testament believer's heart is circumcised by the Word of God when he or she is born again.

The name Gilgal means God has rolled away the reproach of Egypt, which was done by circumcision. So Gilgal is called the place of circumcision. This concept goes right along with New Testament conversion. When one is born again, instead of his foreskin being circumcised, his heart is circumcised.

Romans 2:28-29 (AMP) says "For he is not a real Jew who is only one outwardly and publicly, nor is true circumcision, something external and physical. But he is a Jew who is one inwardly, and true circumcision is of the heart, a spiritual and not a literal matter".

Gilgal is the place where God takes away the reproach of the past. Here God rolled away the reproach of sin from the minister - Joshua 5:9. It is also the place where the minister learns that he is justified by the finished work of Jesus - Romans 5:1-2

So then, in the Gilgal-stage of ministry, young followers are not only born again but are circumcised of the heart. It is here that they will also experience the cutting of the Word of God in their lives, as God cuts away those things that hinder their success in ministry – John 15:2. This may include sinful habits of the pass, financial burdens that would hinder progress in ministry, and associations that would be distractions to training and development in ministry.

Furthermore, circumcision was the prerequisite for the Joshua-generation to crossover the Jordan to the promised land. Just as new-birth (circumcision of the heart) is the perquisite for New Testament believers to go to heaven, it is also a prerequisite for ministering in the Kingdom of God as well – Exodus 12:48-51,

Romans 2:25-29.

Gilgal is also the place where the Passover is observed and the Covenant is renewed. It is where the minister realizes the cleansing power of the blood of the lamb, Jesus Christ - Joshua 5:10-11, and makes a commitment to serve in ministry. Our eligibility for ministry starts the day we are saved. Just as God made provisions for the Israelites once they were circumcised at Gilgal, he does the same for us today as we prepare for ministry.

THE PLACE WHERE MINISTRY BEGINS

Joshua 4:19-24

19 *And the people came up out of Jordan on the tenth day of the first month, and encamped in Gilgal, in the east border of Jericho.*

20 *And those twelve stones, which they took out of Jordan, did Joshua pitch in Gilgal.*

21 *And he spake unto the children of Israel, saying, When your children shall ask their fathers in time to come, saying, What mean these stones?*

22 *Then ye shall let your children know, saying, Israel came over this Jordan on dry land.*

23 *For the LORD your God dried up the waters of Jordan from before you, until ye were passed over, as the LORD your God did to the Red sea, which he dried up from before us, until we were gone over:*

24 *That all the people of the earth might know the hand of the LORD, that it is mighty: that ye might fear the LORD your God for ever.*

Gilgal is the place where ministry begins. The Prophet Elijah takes Elisha home with him to Gilgal. Gilgal calls for building a close relationship at home before ministering abroad. In scripture, it is the place of beginnings.

Gilgal is the place of miraculous provisions for ministry under the leadership of another. It was the place where the Israelites made their entry into the promised-land by the miraculous provisions of God under the leadership of Joshua. It is the memorial site where God congealed the waters of the Jordan so that the Israelites could go across on dry land.

When you have truly obeyed the call of God to enter ministry, you will experience His provisions for you to train and grow, just as Elisha did. Often, your provisions will come in the way of finance for school, arrangement of work hours on your current job so that you can attend Seminary or Bible Training School. He may provide transportation for you to get to and from your place of ministry. He may lay it on the hearts of others to support you with their prayers and finances. He will also supply you with the grace you need to go through and endure the obstacles of training so that you will be thoroughly prepared for ministry.

SETTING UP CAMP

Joshua 4:19
Now the people came up from the Jordan on the tenth day of the first month, and they camped in Gilgal on the East border of Jericho.

Every minister must find a place to settle down, to be subject to the leadership of the one God has placed him or her under. Every Elisha should be able to recognize his or her Elijah, and every Elijah should be able to recognize his or her Elisha. One of the ways to know if you are in a position of Elijah to someone or an Elisha under someone is to look at their revelation of Jesus; as it relates to the vision of the particular ministry that you have been called to.

We have a God-given way for making this determination by

looking at the relationship of Jesus and Peter in Matthew 16:13-19. In this passage Jesus asked his disciples, "Who do you say that I am?", and Peter said, "You are the Christ, the Son of the Living God." Then Jesus said to him, "Flesh and blood did not reveal that to you, but My Father which is in heaven." Jesus went on to say that "upon this Rock (this revelation of Me) I will build my Church and the gates of hell shall not prevail against it". He said, furthermore, "because of your revelation of me, I will give you the keys of the Kingdom of Heaven: and whatever you bind on earth, I will bind in heaven: and whatever you loose of earth, I will lose in heaven."

Notice, there were more disciples there who heard Jesus ask this question, but only Peter answered it. So, he was the one who was granted a special relationship with Jesus because of his revelation of Him. This particular event placed Peter in a different category or rank from his fellow disciples; although any of them could have answered as Peter did. This is also supported by the fact that Jesus said to him "I will give you the keys of the Kingdom of Heaven". My point here is that Peter was promoted spiritually because of his revelation of Jesus. We too, will be promoted spiritually when we attain a greater revelation of Jesus as it relates to our calling in His ministry. That is why it is so important for ministers to prayer and study to show themselves approved of God, workmen need not to be shamed, rightly dividing the Word of truth – 2 Timothy 2:15.

Over the years I have come to the place where I know when I am in the position Elijah or Elisha in a given relationship. It would be good for all ministers to be able to recognize what position they hold in any given relationship. I can meet another man of God and discern right away which position I am in by virtue of our communication and interaction. So often this lack of recognizing or discerning which position we are in causes unnecessary delays and confusion within the Body of Christ. This lack of discernment often causes us to miss what God had intended for an individual; and in some cases the entire local church.

Many times "the Word" God has for a particular group of believers does not get taught or preached because of this lack of recognition. In some cases, there is a flat out denial or lack of recognition that a particular ministry gift is at hand. This often occurs because of man-made requirements for ministry - such as a minister has not been formally given a particular title or recognition within a given body of believers. Or, those in leadership do not have the level of discernment to hear what Holy Spirit may be saying in a given situation; especially when such prompting or discernment is contrary to what has already been scheduled or planned. If you are a minister who is submitted to your leadership and remain under authority at all times, God will promote you to where you need to be.

TESTIMONY AND COMMEMORATION

Joshua 4:20-24

20 *And those twelve stones which they took out of the Jordan, Joshua set up in Gilgal.*

21 *Then he spoke to the children of Israel, saying: "When your children (biological or spiritual) ask their fathers in time to come, saying, 'What are these stones'?*

22 *"then you shall let your children know, saying, 'Israel crossed over this Jordan on dry land';*

23 *"for the LORD your God dried up the waters of the Jordan before you until you had crossed over, as the LORD your God did to the Red Sea, which He dried up before us until we had crossed over,*

24 *"that all the peoples of the earth may know the hand of the* LORD, *that it is mighty, that you may fear the* LORD *your God forever."*

This is also true for the New Testament Minister, Gilgal should be the place of your testimony; how God saved you and placed you into the ministry of His Son Jesus Christ. You too, should have stones of testimony that commemorate how God translated you out of the kingdom of darkness and into the kingdom of His dear son, Jesus Christ. Your testimony is the one thing that no one can ever take from you. It is one of your more effective tools for winning others to Christ. By sharing your testimony, you are able to put your passion and sincerity into it. This ingredient will always work for you during times of altar call or just witnessing to someone on the street.

THE PLACE OF GUIDANCE AND AFFIRMATION

1 Samuel 10:8 13

8 *"You shall go down before me to Gilgal; and surely I will come down to you to offer burnt offerings and make sacrifices of peace offerings. Seven days you shall wait, till I come to you and show you what you should do."*

9 *So it was, when he had turned his back to go from Samuel, that God gave him another heart; and all those signs came to pass that day.*

10 *When they came there to the hill, there was a group of prophets to meet him; then the Spirit of God came upon him, and he prophesied among them.*

11 *And it happened, when all who knew him formerly saw that he indeed prophesied among the prophets, that the people said to one another, "What is this that has come upon the son of Kish? Is Saul also among the prophets?"*

12 *Then a man from there answered and said, "But who is their father?" Therefore it became a proverb: "Is Saul also among the prophets?"*

13 *And when he had finished prophesying, he went to the high place.*

Here Samuel instructed Saul to meet him in Gilgal. It was there that Samuel confirmed that Saul was chosen by God to be the King over Israel. He also gave him guidance on his new position in the Kingdom of God and directions for what he was to do after their meeting. When Saul left Samuel and proceeded to carry out his instructions, other prophets also confirmed that Saul indeed was the anointed of God.

The same is true for you. You will be given guidance and instructions from those God has place in your life. They will help to guide you into what he has for you. They will also confirm your new position in the Kingdom of God. God will not leave you wondering about His call on your life.

Going in the ministry is not some haphazard journey you are to take without fully understanding what God wants you to do. God will always speak to you from His Word and by Holy Spirit. He may also speak to you through mature ministers and believers to provide you with guidance in ministry. Most often He uses mature ministers and believers to confirm what he has already spoken to you. That is why it is so important for you to develop the inner ear to hear Holy Spirit. John 4:24 says that God is a Spirit and those that worship Him must worship him in Spirit and in truth. Because God is Spirit, He will speak to you in your spirit. Your spirit was made alive by Holy Spirit when you were born again. At new birth, God's Spirit came into your spirit. Your spirit became His sanctuary. He is there in you but you will have to get to know and understand His voice just as young Samuel did in 1 Samuel 3:4-10. With the help of a seasoned and mature minister, Samuel learned to hear God's voice. Your Elijah (the minister or leader you are under) should be a seasoned and mature minister who teaches you to hear the voice of God.

Manna that Comes in a Different Manner

Joshua 5:10 12

10 *So the children of Israel camped in Gilgal, and kept the Passover on the fourteenth day of the month at twilight on the plains of Jericho.*

11 *And they ate of the produce of the land on the day after the Passover, unleavened bread and parched grain, on the very same day.*

12 *Then the manna ceased on the day after they had eaten the produce of the land; and the children of Israel no longer had manna, but they ate the food of the land of Canaan that year.*

Gilgal is the place where the minister learns to feed himself and live by the Gospel - Joshua 5:10-12, 2 Timothy 2:15. God stopped feeding the Israelites manna at Gilgal. From that point on, they had to learn to eat from the land they conquered. When the manna stops, the minister must learn to eat of the land that he conquers. You must understand that the manna will now come in a different manner. A baby is given milk in its infantile stage of development, and as it grows in maturity and in ability to get its own food, the parent no longer has to hand-feed it. It is the same with you and God. When you first got saved, you were a babe in Christ and God saw to it that you were nourished by others from His Word. They also taught you how to receive from Him through Holy Spirit. Your food came easy. You received insights about the kingdom of God and you were motivated and encouraged by that food. But now that you are older and capable of going to the Word and feeding yourself, you will no longer be hand-fed by God. You will still receive revelations and insights from God, but they will come through your diligent study of the Word and through prayer and fasting. Know this - what you will be getting by your own efforts will still be superb manna from God, only you will receive it in a different manner. You will have a greater appreciation for it because you worked for it. Proverbs 13:4 says that the soul of the diligent shall be made fat. Proverbs 10:4 says that the hand of the diligent shall be made rich. Yes, you can get rich manna from God in abundance when you work for it.

Ministers should also partake of the altar of God by the gospel they preach - I Corinthians 9:13, 14. Although Joshua and the children of Israel physically conquered the land before them, with the help of God, the New Testament believer conquers through prayer by faith. This is where your faith in God becomes very vital to your success in ministry. As a minister of the Gospel, you must learn to live by faith and not by sight. Romans 1:17 says that the just shall live by faith. To put it into laymen terms, the justified know that they are entitled to what they need in the kingdom of God. They know that the cattle on a thousand hills belong to God. They know that all the gold and silver belongs to God. They know that they can ask and it will be given to them. They know that they can seek and will find. They know that they can knock and the door will be opened for them – Luke 11:9-10. They know that God has a vast altar that encompasses all that they will ever need. They know that they have a place on God's altar. So, they present themselves as living sacrifices on that altar and call for those things that they need. Even though they don't see those things initially, they keep calling for them as if they were there, until they are actually there – Romans 4:17.

The Bethel Ministry

Ministering under the covering of another
Follow-ship that leads to Leader-ship

STAGE TWO

Followers should minister at Bethel. Bethel is the Second Stage of Mantel Ministry. It is the place where the minister learns to minister in the House of God - 2 Kings 2:2-3 & Acts 1:8, Genesis 28:17

THE HOUSE OF GOD

2 Kings 2:2-3
2 *And Elijah said unto Elisha, Tarry here, I pray thee; for the LORD hath sent me to Bethel. And Elisha said unto him, As the LORD liveth, and as thy soul liveth, I will not leave thee. So they went down to Bethel.*
3 *And the sons of the prophets that were at Bethel came forth to Elisha, and said unto him, Knowest thou that the LORD will take away thy master from thy head to day? And he said, Yea, I know it; hold ye your peace.*

Jacob called the place where he saw the gate of heaven

open to him the house of **God**, which is the word "'**Bethel**" in the Hebrew language. Thus, Bethel is called the house of God. It is where the minister learns to work inside God's house. Elisha goes with Elijah to the House of God and stays there with him to learn from Elijah. Whatever Elijah did, Elisha did. Wherever Elijah went, Elisha went. He was always there to serve Elijah; to pour water on his hands or to give him a cool cup of water. He became totally committed to him and became his understudy. Elisha was not swayed by other opportunities because he knew that God had placed him in the House of God to learn the things of God from the man of God. In 2 Kings 2:2 Elisha said to Elijah, "As my soul lives I will not leave you." I call this a soul-tie. We see that Elisha is willing to serve Elijah with all of his soul – with all of his mind, will and emotions because he is doing it as unto God. I call this true commitment and loyalty beyond reproach.

You too should find your Elijah and stay with him in the House of God to learn the things of God. For you to get a double portion of the anointing of God, you will have to give all of you to the ministry - all of your mind, will and emotion. You should know that God placed you under your Elijah's leadership. You should know that God has given your Elijah everything you need to become an anointed, humble and effective minister of the Gospel. But you will have to stay the course to reap the blessings of the anointing God has placed on your Elijah, just as Elisha did.

THE GATEWAY TO GOD

Genesis 28:10-22

10 And Jacob went out from Beersheba, and went toward Haran.

11 And he lighted upon a certain place, and tarried there all night, because the sun was set; and he took of the stones of that place, and put *them for his pillows, and lay down in that place to sleep.*

12 *And he dreamed, and behold a ladder set up on the earth, and the top of it reached to heaven: and behold the angels of God ascending and descending on it.*

13 *And, behold, the LORD stood above it, and said, I am the LORD God of Abraham thy father, and the God of Isaac: the land whereon thou liest, to thee will I give it, and to thy seed;*

14 *And thy seed shall be as the dust of the earth, and thou shalt spread abroad to the west, and to the east, and to the north, and to the south: and in thee and in thy seed shall all the families of the earth be blessed.*

15 *And, behold, I am with thee, and will keep thee in all places whither thou goest, and will bring thee again into this land; for I will not leave thee, until I have done that which I have spoken to thee of.*

16 *And Jacob awaked out of his sleep, and he said, Surely the LORD is in this place; and I knew it not.*

17 *And he was afraid, and said, How dreadful is this place! this is none other but the house of God, and this is the gate of heaven.*

18 *And Jacob rose up early in the morning, and took the stone that he had put for his pillows, and set it up for a pillar, and poured oil upon the top of it.*

19 *And he called the name of that place Bethel: but the name of that city was called Luz at the first.*

20 *And Jacob vowed a vow, saying, If God will be with me, and will keep me in this way that I go, and will give me bread to eat, and raiment to put on,*

21 *So that I come again to my father's house in peace; then shall the LORD be my God:*

22 *And this stone, which I have set for a pillar, shall be God's house: and of all that thou shalt give me I will surely give the tenth unto thee.*

Just as it was for Jacob, Bethel is the gateway to God for you.

It is the place where you develop a special relationship with God. No matter what you do, just like Jacob, you will not be able to shake your Bethel experience with God. This gateway experience will become a guiding beacon for you. It will lead you back to Bethel time and time again for yet another experience with God that is greater than the time before – Genesis 28:17, Genesis 35:1, 7, 10, 14.

You should come to realize that the Gate of Heaven is open to you in the house of God. Your Bethel is where you see the gate of heaven open to you. You should be thankful for your Bethel and give God the tenth of all that he gives you through the bethel gate – Genesis 28:22.

Jesus introduced his disciples to the Bethel ministry, which he called the Kingdom. Like the disciples of Jesus, ministers should learn to distinguish tares from wheat and know how to deal with false believers in a way that does not root up the true believers in the Kingdom – Matthew 13:24. They should learn the power and potential of the Word of God while living in a world that regards it as a mustard seed – Matthew 13:31. They should learn to wait on the transforming power of the unseen work of Holy Spirit and the Word of God in seemingly impossible situations and circumstances – Matthew 13:33. They should be sold out to the ministry of Jesus Christ and walk in the joy of knowing the price of that prize – Matthew 13:44, 45.

Furthermore, ministers should learn to cast their nets for souls and gather them for the Kingdom of God – Matthew 13:47. They should learn to bring forth both old and new things from the Treasury of God's Word for the people of God – Matthew 13:52. They should learn to operate in godly precepts, principles and laws in a sinful world, and adjust their attitudes with the beatitudes of the Kingdom of God – Matthew 5:3-12. They should learn that the Blood of Jesus has broken down the middle wall of partition between all men – Ephesians 2:11-18, 19-22. They should readily understand that it's not their ministry; it belongs to Jesus Christ who is King over His own Kingdom – Hebrews 3:1-6.

THE PLACE OF VISION

Bethel is the place where God gives the minister a heavenly vision that will set his or her destiny in ministry - Genesis 28:10-14; 35:1, 7, 10, 14. It was here that God gave Jacob a vision of what he would become and how his descendants would be as the dust of the earth, spread abroad to the West, East, North and South; and that all the families of the earth would be blessed by them. All that Jacob would do from that point on would be shaped by this vision. He is the carrier of the "Blessing" of God for all the families of the earth. This was the same vision that God had given to his Fathers, Isaac and Abraham in Genesis 26:2-5; 12:1-3. Even though they lived at different times and in different circumstances, the vision remained the same. And the same is true for you; at your Bethel God will give you His vision of "Blessing" which is salvation for you, your seed and all nations of the world – Genesis 28:12-14.

Whatever vision God gives to you, no matter the times or circumstances, it will be the same vision that he gave to Abraham, then to Isaac and Jacob, and on down to Jesus. It is the vision of the Blessing of salvation for mankind. That is why He sent His Son Jesus Christ as Savior of the world – John 3:16. Even though you may get it a little different than Jacob, your vision should line-up with God ultimate plan of salvation. Isn't it amazing how God passes the same vision, from generation to generation, and then to you? Yes, He is an Amazing God!

You may hear and see visions that seem to be unique to a particular ministry, but if it's of God, it will always point to the Blessing of Salvation through Jesus Christ.   That is why all vision must fall under the ministry of Jesus Christ. It is never your own personal ministry. It is always the ministry of Jesus!

THE PLACE OF PROVISION

Just as Jacob was assured of God's provision for him at Bethel, you should know that God will personally assure you of His provisions for you in ministry - Genesis 28:15. Notice that when God assured Jacob that He would be with him and provide for him, Jacob then began to walk by faith in what God had said to him. With his faith in God's Word, he goes into a new land. There he encounters new people and uncertain circumstances, but his confidence in God never falters.   In fact, he becomes very enterprising and ultimately becomes wealthy because of his abiding faith in God's ability to provide for him – see Genesis, Chapters 29-31.

THE PLACE OF RELEVANCE

It is very important that you come to see the relevance of your earthly minister to its heavenly origin.   This means that you are to minister on earth for a heavenly cause. Although the laws, principles and precepts you will be employing will be from a heavenly kingdom, they can be very effective on earth when you understand that you are the mediator between heaven and earth. Bethel should be the place where the minister clearly sees a heaven and earth relationship in ministry - Genesis 28:12.

THE PLACE OF REVELATION

Bethel is the place where God reveals Himself to the minister in a special way - Genesis 28:12-13; 35:6-7. It was at Bethel that God gave Jacob his identity and assured him that He would be with him wherever he went. Jacob would later return to his Bethel after seeing his God provide for him and protect him. Now he calls it El-bethel, which is to say in the Hebrew language, the house where God dwells. Bethel became the hallmark of Jacob's faith. Like Jacob, your Bethel should become the hallmark of your faith in God.

The Jericho Ministry

Ministering under the covering of another
Follow-ship that leads to Leader-ship

STAGE THREE

Jericho is the Third Stage of Mantle Ministry. It is the place of confirmation and confrontation. Elisha received his second confirmation of his place in ministry at Jericho, and Joshua, who was a minister to Moses fought and won a great battle at Jericho.

2 Kings 2:5
And the sons of the prophets that were at Jericho came to Elisha, and said unto him, Knowest thou that the LORD will take away thy master from thy head today? And he answered, Yea, I know it; hold ye your peace.

Joshua 6:1-5
1 Now Jericho was straitly shut up because of the children of Israel: none went out, and none came in.
2 And the LORD said unto Joshua, See, I have given into thine hand Jericho, and the king thereof, and the mighty men of valour.
3 And ye shall compass the city, all ye men of war, and go round about the city once. Thus shalt thou do six days.

4 And seven priests shall bear before the ark seven trumpets of rams' horns: and the seventh day ye shall compass the city seven times, and the priests shall blow with the trumpets.

5 And it shall come to pass, that when they make a long blast with the ram's horn, and when ye hear the sound of the trumpet, all the people shall shout with a great shout; and the wall of the city shall fall down flat, and the people shall ascend up every man straight before him.

Joshua 6:13-16

13 And seven priests bearing seven trumpets of rams' horns before the ark of the LORD went on continually, and blew with the trumpets: and the armed men went before them; but the rereward came after the ark of the LORD, the priests going on, and blowing with the trumpets.

14 And the second day they compassed the city once, and returned into the camp: so they did six days.

15 And it came to pass on the seventh day, that they rose early about the dawning of the day, and compassed the city after the same manner seven times: only on that day they compassed the city seven times.

16 And it came to pass at the seventh time, when the priests blew with the trumpets, Joshua said unto the people, Shout; for the LORD hath given you the city.

Jericho is the place where the minister learns the power of praise and the rewards of faith-praise, which is to praise God before the victory - Joshua 6:1-5, 15-16. It is at Jericho that the minister learns godly strategies for defeating the enemy.

Captain of Host

Joshua 5:5

Now all the people that came out were circumcised: but all the people

that were born in the wilderness by the way as they came forth out of Egypt,
them they had not circumcised.

Joshua 5:13-15

13 And it came to pass, when Joshua was by Jericho, that he lifted up
his eyes and looked, and, behold, there stood a man over against him with
his sword drawn in his hand: and Joshua went unto him, and said unto him,
Art thou for us, or for our adversaries?

14 And he said, Nay; but as captain of the host of the LORD am I now
come. And Joshua fell on his face to the earth, and did worship, and said
unto him, What saith my Lord unto his servant?

15 And the captain of the LORD's host said unto Joshua, Loose thy
shoe from off thy foot; for the place whereon thou standest is holy. And
Joshua did so.

In Joshua 5:5, 13-14, we see that Jericho is the place where
ministers learn to worship and revere the Captain of the Host. We
know from the whole council of scripture that Jesus is the Captain
of the Host that is depicted here. Therefore it is here at Jericho
that ministers get a greater revelation of who Jesus is and His
readiness to fight the enemies of those who are on God's side.
They come to understand that their worship of the Captain of the
host prepares them to receive vital instructions on how to take
the stronghold of the enemy. They learn that circumcision comes
before the revelation of Captain of the host, and worship of Him
comes before His release of His power to defeat their enemies.
They also learn that Jericho is the place where Holy-Ground
Consecration comes before victory in battle - Joshua 5:15.

Shout the Victory

Joshua 6:14-16

14 And the second day they compassed the city once, and returned into the camp: so they did six days.

15 And it came to pass on the seventh day, that they rose early about the dawning of the day, and compassed the city after the same manner seven times: only on that day they compassed the city seven times.

16 And it came to pass at the seventh time, when the priests blew with the trumpets, Joshua said unto the people, Shout; for the LORD hath given you the city.

At Jericho ministers learn to shout for victory. They learn that high praise is as a two-edge sword and that God-ordained praise is their strength - Joshua 6:14-16, Psalm 149, Psalm 8:2, Matthew 21:16. They learn that praise causes God to come where they are – Psalm 22:3-4

Keeping the Curse out of the Camp

Joshua 6:18

And ye, in any wise keep yourselves from the accursed thing, lest ye make yourselves accursed, when ye take of the accursed thing, and make the camp of Israel a curse, and trouble it.

At Jericho the ministers learn to keep themselves from the accursed things. They learn that if they partake of sin, it will eventually bring the curse on them and on the house where they serve - Joshua 6:18.

Discerning Resources

Joshua 6:19

But all the silver, and gold, and vessels of brass and iron, are consecrated unto the LORD: they shall come into the treasury of the LORD.

At Jericho ministers learn what resources are to be used in the work of the ministry. They learn to put praise out front, make it the first thing they do when faced with bearers or walls that prevent ministry from going forth as God intends for it to go.

Judah-Praise

Genesis 29:35

And she conceived again and bore a son, and said, "Now I will praise the LORD." Therefore she called his name Judah. Then she stopped bearing.

Genesis 49:8

Judah, you are he whom your brothers shall praise; Your hand shall be on the neck of your enemies; Your father's children shall bow down before you.

Judges 1:1-4

1 Now after the death of Joshua it came to pass that the children of Israel asked the LORD, saying, "Who shall be first to go up for us against the Canaanites to fight against them?"

2 And the LORD said, "Judah shall go up. Indeed I have delivered the land into his hand."

3 So Judah said to Simeon his brother, "Come up with me to my allotted territory, that we may fight against the Canaanites; and I will likewise go with you to your allotted territory." And Simeon went with him.

4 Then Judah went up, and the LORD delivered the Canaanites and the Perizzites into their hand; and they killed ten thousand men at Bezek.

Judges 20:18

Then the children of Israel arose and went up to the house of God to inquire of God. They said, "Which of us shall go up first to battle against the children of Benjamin?" The LORD said, "Judah first!"

Revelation 5:5

But one of the elders said to me, "Do not weep. Behold, the Lion of the tribe of Judah, the Root of David, has prevailed to open the scroll and to loose its seven seals."

When we take into account the scriptures above, we can see that in Genesis 29:35, the name Judah means Praise the Lord. After Leah had her 4th male child, she praised the Lord for that child; and to capture that moment, she named the child Judah, which means "Praise the Lord".

You will find in scripture that God, in His sovereign providence, often uses the names of biblical characters to promote the agenda of his Kingdom and to fulfill prophecy. We can see this when we read Genesis 49:8 and compare it with Revelation 5:5. It becomes clear that God spoke prophetically through Jacob when he prophesized that Judah's bothers would praise him, and that his hand would be on the neck of his enemies, and that he would be over his bothers.

In Judges 1:1-4 and Judges 20:18, we see were God tells the Israelites to send **Judah first** when they had to go into battle. When they obeyed God they were victorious over their enemies.

These Old Testament prophecies, as well as the very practice of the Israelites in battle, are foreshadows of Jesus Christ our Lord and Savior. He is indeed the Lion of Judah. He is indeed Lord over His brothers; the born again believers. He has and will put His hand on his and our enemies' neck when we praise Him. All of this leads to my main point, which is, **Judah-Praise** is to **Praise-Jesus-First** before we go into battle with our enemies. Praising Jesus first is the same as sending Jesus first against our enemies. Then we are sure to win the battle every time.

Please note that chapters 5 and 6 of the book Joshua are all about the power of praise. The priests that Joshua had go before them blowing their horns are symbolic of New Testament praise by the born again believer. They did it in the natural and we do it in the power of Holy Spirit. Their weapon against their enemies was the shout of the mouth by the priests of the Tribe of Judah. Our weapon against our enemies is the shout of our praise to Jesus, the Lion of Judah – Glory!

So then, at Jericho ministers learn that first-praise is **Judah-Praise**, and that Judah-Praise is to praise Jesus, the true Lion of Judah. They come to understand that Judah-Praise is ordained praise that God inhabits – Psalm 22:3. They soon learn that when they praised Jesus He puts His hand on the neck of their enemies. They learn to employ praise as an offensive weapon against their enemies. They learn to identify those who are priests of praise and put them out front before they wage war against their enemies. They come to understand that the power of praise defeats their enemies just as Joshua and the Israelites defeated theirs at Jericho - Joshua 6:16.

At Jericho ministers learn that first-praise is Judah-Praise. They come to understand that Judah-Praise is to praise Jesus, the Lion of Judah. They come to understand that Judah-Praise is ordained praise that God inhabits. They soon learn that when Judah is praised by his brothers, He puts His feet on the neck of their enemy - Genesis 29:35; 49:8, Revelation 5:5.

They also learn to employ praise as an offensive weapon and to identify those who are priests of praise and put them out front. They understand the role of praise in defeating the enemy - Joshua 6:16.

Conquering Strongholds

Jericho is the place where the ministers learn to bring down the walls of the enemy's strongholds and evangelize the conquered territory - Joshua 6:20-23, 25. They learn that the weapons of their warfare are mighty through God and are able to pull down strongholds and every high thing that exalts itself against the knowledge of God. They learn that they can bring every thought under the captivity of the name of Jesus.

Here they learn to appreciate what praise can do to a Jericho wall that looks impossible to bring down. To put things into perspective, the shout of the Israelites, led by Joshua, brought down the Jericho wall, which was a double-wall that was composed of an outer wall and an inner wall. The outer wall and inner wall were constructed 15 feet apart. The outer wall was six feet thick and the inner wall was 12 feet thick. Both walls where 30 feet high. This wall was wide enough for Rehab's house to rest upon it. By their shout, this wall fell into the earth vertically. In other words, it was pushed into the earth because they obeyed Joshua's instructions to shout. Just as the Israelites brought down their Jericho Wall by following Joshua's leadership, you too can learn to bring down the Jericho Walls in your life by following the leadership of your Elijah.

The dimensions of the Jericho Wall are symbolic of two things for the believer; the stronghold of the enemy against us, and the stronghold of the fleshly nature within us. While Jesus Christ has conquered the stronghold of the enemy against us, we have to learn to cooperate with Holy Spirit and other believers to conquer the strongholds within us. Ministers should come to see that this is a picture of God's ability to bring down strongholds within them as they cooperate with Him as He prepares them for ministry.

Therefore, with God's help, at Jericho ministers should conquer the stronghold of character flaws in their lives. We only have to look at the past and contemporary history of the Christian Church to see glaring examples of men and women who fell short of the mark. These men and women had a calling from God on their lives with a great anointing to carry it out. Unfortunately, they brought shame and dismay to themselves and their followers because they never dealt with their character flaws. Just when they were at the pinnacle of their ministry, their character flaws destroyed them. We must not play games with ourselves, or hide our inner struggles from those we are accountable to. We all are subject to weaknesses of the flesh because of the fall of Adam in the Garden of Eden.

The most vital thing we can do while we are in the Jericho stage of ministry is to deal with our character flaws. There is no such thing as a perfect person. If we could be perfect on our own, Jesus would not have come to die for our sins and give us new life. There is no such thing as a professional Christian. Yes, we do mature as Christians, but we will never be able to live the Christian life out of our own strength. While new life has come to our spirit or spirit-man, our flesh or natural- man is still subject to the weaknesses of the flesh.

Therefore, we will always be dependent on Jesus and His

grace that enables us to carry out the will of our Father God. That is why Paul wrote Galatians 2:20, which says " I am crucified with Christ: nevertheless I live; yet not I, but Christ lives in me: and the life that I now live in the flesh I live by the faith of the Son of God, who loved me, and gave Himself for me". On the other hand, James 5:16 says "Confess your faults one to another, and pray one for another, that you might be healed. The effectual fervent prayer of a righteous man avails much." From these two verses, we can see our need to be dependent on Jesus and our need to confess our faults to other mature believers so that we can get healed of or delivered from those faults.

Many churches and some bible training schools conduct special encounter sessions where a few believers gather with senior believers who have been trained to help others overcome personal faults or strongholds of the flesh in their lives. Ministers in the Jericho stage of ministry should attend such an encounter to overcome strongholds or character flaws in their lives. There, they can deal with their faults or inner struggles in the confines of a special setting that is designed to provide them with guidance and counsel by a staff of mature believers. In such a setting, ministers can deal with personal struggles such as sexual lust, gambling, pornography, homosexuality, lesbianism, mishandling of money, and many other types of fleshly strongholds that could be a problem for them later in their ministry.

To put it in a nutshell, I have been told by my elders that ministers should stay away from the 3Gs; that is, the Gals (or Guys if you are a female), the Gold, and the Glory. These 3Gs seem to sum up the many ways that ministers can be pulled away from their steadfastness in the Lord. Obviously, it is a little more complex than that, but the 3Gs help you to remember that you should: stay away from the opposite sex or the same sex in the wrong context – 2 Timothy 2:22, take the necessary precautions to ensure you do not mishandle money – 1 Timothy 6:10, and keep your pride in check and always give God the glory for what He does in you and through you – Isaiah 42:8; 48:11.

The Jordan Ministry

Ministering under the covering of another
Follow-ship that leads to Leader-ship

STAGE FOUR

2 Kings 2:6-14

6 Then Elijah said to him, "Stay here, please, for the LORD has sent me on to the Jordan."

But he said, "As the LORD lives, and as your soul lives, I will not leave you!" So the two of them went on.

7 And fifty men of the sons of the prophets went and stood facing them at a distance, while the two of them stood by the Jordan.

8 Now Elijah took his mantle, rolled it up, and struck the water; and it was divided this way and that, so that the two of them crossed over on dry ground.

9 And so it was, when they had crossed over, that Elijah said to Elisha, "Ask! What may I do for you, before I am taken away from you?"

Elisha said, "Please let a double portion of your spirit be upon me."

10 So he said, "You have asked a hard thing. Nevertheless, if you see me when I am taken from you, it shall be so for you; but if not, it shall not be so."

11 Then it happened, as they continued on and talked, that suddenly *a chariot of fire appeared with horses of fire, and separated the two of them; and Elijah went up by a whirlwind into heaven.*

12 *And Elisha saw it, and he cried out, "My father, my father, the chariot of Israel and its horsemen!" So he saw him no more. And he took hold of his own clothes and tore them into two pieces.*

13 *He also took up the mantle of Elijah that had fallen from him, and went back and stood by the bank of the Jordan.*

14 *Then he took the mantle of Elijah that had fallen from him, and struck the water, and said, "Where is the LORD God of Elijah?" And when he also had struck the water, it was divided this way and that; and Elisha crossed over.*

Jordan is the Fourth and Final Stage of Mantle Ministry. It is the place where followers become leaders. It is the place where they come into the fullness of the gifts of Holy Spirit. It is also the place where they learn to bear the presence of God and recognize their priestly position to lead others into God's presence.

TAKING UP THE MANTLE

2 Kings 2:8
Now Elijah took his mantle, rolled it up, and struck the water; and it was divided this way and that, so that the two of them crossed over on dry ground.

Jordan is the place where the minister learns to part the waters. Notice that Elisha took the mantle of Elijah and struck the waters of Jordan to see if he had the same anointing that Elijah had. And just like Elijah, the waters parted for him and he went over to the other side. The Jordan Stage of your ministry is when your will get your opportunity to test the mantle of your

73

Elijah. Now it is time for you to test the mantle you have caught from your Elijah. You have been there with your Elijah until the time of your season. Your proximity (closeness) to your Elijah has allowed you to catch his anointing.

THE DOUBLE PORTION

2 Kings 2:9-12

9 *And so it was, when they had crossed over, that Elijah said to Elisha, "Ask! What may I do for you, before I am taken away from you?"*
Elisha said, "Please let a double portion of your spirit be upon me."

At the Jordan Elisha asked for a double portion of Elijah's spirit. Elijah's spirit was anointed by God because God is anointed. One definition of anointing is to smear or to rub off. Elijah was known for his intimate relationship with God and he spent lots of time with Him throughout his ministry. When you spend time with someone who is anointed, his anointing will rub off on you. At your Jordan stage of ministry, the anointing of your Elijah should have rubbed off on you, if you stayed close to him. Now it's time for your double portion. If your Elijah was anointed to preach, you will be anointed to preach twice–as–good. If he was an anointed teacher, you will be anointed to teach twice–as–good. If he was an evangelist, you will be an evangelist, only twice–as–good. You have been with him until the time of your season and now it is time for you to operate in the full gifting(s) of your calling.

If you would do a careful study of the life of Elijah and Elisha, you would find that Elijah performed sixteen miracles during his life. You would also discover that Elisha performed thirty-one miracles during his life time and one from his grave. You see a dead man was thrown into it Elisha's grave by a band of thieves.

As soon as the dead man touched Elisha's bones he was revived, became alive again. This miracle completed the double portion anointing that Elisha originally asked for - 2 Kings 13:20-21. This shows God's faithfulness to us. Even after we have transitioned from earth to heaven, He makes good his promises to us.

You should also keep in mind that Elisha is alive in heaven, because God is not the God of the dead but of the living. Matthew 22:32 verifies this and Matthew 17:1-3 shows Moses, who had died physically and Elijah who was suddenly taken to heaven by the chariot and horses of fire, appear alive with Jesus on the mountain when he was transfigured. So, you see that Elisha was able to observe his "Bone-Miracle" from heaven. Glory to God!

LIKE FATHER, LIKE SON

1 Corinthians 4:15
For though you might have ten thousand instructors in Christ, yet you do not have many fathers; for in Christ Jesus I have begotten you through the gospel.

Notice that Elisha's proximity (closeness) to Elijah allowed him to catch his mantle of anointing. Elijah then carried the title of father and Elisha became his spiritual-son. Because of your proximity to your Elijah, you will catch his mantle of anointing and will be his spiritual-son. This is a spiritual expression of the term "like father, like son".

THE DOUBLE PORTION FOR YOU AND ME

Notice that Elisha was promised a double portion of Elijah's anointing. But, first he made a quality decision to follow Elijah and was totally committed to him and his ministry. Because of his close proximity to Elijah, he received an inner training that developed his love for Elijah and his faith in his ministry. This training also developed Elisha's character, patience and endurance. These are all good qualities that believers should have today. The New Testament believers should get similar training when they are born again. Although Elisha had the inner substance of his experience with Elijah, he did not have the outer power to execute the spiritual gifting(s) to perform the miracles that Elijah performed, that is, until he caught Elijah's mantle. Once he caught Elijah's mantle he was able to do the miracles that Elijah had done.

Jesus said in John 14:2 that his disciples would do greater works than He did because he was going to the Father. Then in Luke 24:49, He told them that he would send the promise of the Father upon them, but they were to wait in the city of Jerusalem until they were endued with power from on high. And in Acts 2, on the day of Pentecost, we see the Promise of the Father coming upon the disciples and they were filled with Holy Spirit and began to speak with other tongues as He gave them utterance.

The double portion Elisha received is a precursor to New Testament Salvation and Baptism of the Holy Spirit for the believer. As I have discussed in chapter 4, the Holy Spirit is Jesus' mantle to us, the born again believers. Like Elijah, Jesus allowed His mantle to fall upon His followers on the Day of Pentecost. From that point on, in the book of Acts, we see people being saved and filled with the Holy Spirit. I submit to you that this is the Double Portion that God has provided for every believer who is a follower of Jesus Christ. When Holy Spirit comes upon you, you will be able to do doubly what your Elijah has done. Like Jesus said in Acts 1:8, you will receive this power after Holy

Spirit comes upon you, and you will be His witness, ministering at home, in your community, in your state or region and beyond.

Notice that your ministry should first begin at home. Your family becomes your followers. You are in the Elijah position to your family. And like the Prophet Elijah, your ministry will be to turn your heart to your children, and your children will turn their hearts to you; so that you can lead them away from the curse to the blessings of God. The same ministry you provide for your immediate family will be the model you will use to lead your spiritual children in your community, in your state and beyond, to the blessings of God - Malachi 4:6.

THE PLACE OF PROMOTION

2 Kings 2:8
Now Elijah took his mantle, rolled it up, and struck the water; and it was divided this way and that, so that the two of them crossed over on dry ground.

2 Kings 2:11-13
11 Then it happened, as they continued on and talked, that suddenly a chariot of fire appeared with horses of fire, and separated the two of them; and Elijah went up by a whirlwind into heaven.

12 And Elisha saw it, and he cried out, "My father, my father, the chariot of Israel and its horsemen!" So he saw him no more. And he took hold of his own clothes and tore them into two pieces.

13 He also took up the mantle of Elijah that had fallen from him, and went back and stood by the bank of the Jordan.

Jordan is the place of elevation and promotion. Elisha was promoted to leadership when Elijah was taken up to heaven. This all occurred on the far side of Jordan. Elisha was able to catch Elijah's mantle, part the waters of the Jordan and return to the other side.

We can see from this passage of scripture that when the leader is promoted, the follower is also promoted. Elisha was promoted out of his faithfulness to Elijah. He was willing to follow Elijah wherever he went. He continued to serve Elijah until he was promoted. This all occurred when Elisha least expected it. But when it happened, Elisha was right where he needed to be to catch the falling mantle of Elijah. If you remain faithful to your Elijah and stay with him or her until promotion time, you too will be there to catch the mantle of your Elijah. If he is an anointed teacher or preacher, you will catch that anointing. But you will have the potential to be twice as anointed as he was. The student should always excel beyond his or her teacher. Generally, you will find in scripture that the younger one is in a better position for success than his predecessor was. We see this with Esau and Jacob, Joseph and his elder brothers and Jesus and Adam. That is why Jesus is called the second Adam.

THE MANTLE TEST

2 Kings 2:13-14

13 *He also took up the mantle of Elijah that had fallen from him, and went back and stood by the bank of the Jordan.*

14 *Then he took the mantle of Elijah that had fallen from him, and struck the water, and said, "Where is the LORD God of Elijah?" And when he also had struck the water, it was divided this way and that; and Elisha crossed over.*

Jordan is the place where your mantle-gift is tested and

proven. Note that Elisha caught Elijah's mantle on the far side of the river. Just prior to Elijah being taken, both he and Elijah had gone across the Jordan River after Elijah parted it with his mantle. After Elisha caught the mantle, he had to test it to see if he had the same anointing that Elijah had. He then took Elijah's mantle and struck the waters and they parted for him just as they did for Elijah. He then went across the Jordan to launch his ministry of leadership for other prophets.

Once your Elijah is promoted, you too will have an opportunity to test your new mantle. Your new mantle will carry you over your Jordan and launch you into leadership. Your mantle will make room for you. In other words, what you obtained from your relationship with your Elijah will equip you to be an effective leader of others and you will be recognized for your leadership expertise.

THE MANTLE OF LEADERSHIP

2 Kings 2:15
Now when the sons of the prophets who were from Jericho saw him, they said, "The spirit of Elijah rests on Elisha." And they came to meet him, and bowed to the ground before him.

At Jordan others will recognize your mantle of leadership and the anointing God has placed on your life. They will come to you and submit themselves to your God-given authority. Just as your Elijah was a father to you, you will have the opportunity to be a father to those who follow you. You will be able to train and guide them in ministry just as Elijah trained and guided you in ministry.

BEARERS OF GOD'S PRESENCE

Joshua 3:3-4

3 *And they commanded the people, saying, When ye see the ark of the covenant of the LORD your God, and the priests the Levites bearing it, then ye shall remove from your place, and go after it.*

4 *Yet there shall be a space between you and it, about two thousand cubits by measure: come not near unto it, that ye may know the way by which ye must go: for ye have not passed this way heretofore.*

The Ark of Covenant represents God's presence. In the Old Testament God would appear on the Mercy Seat of the Ark of Covenant and commune with the High Priest while he was conducting service to Him in presenting the blood of a lamb on the behalf of the Israelites and himself. In the New Testament, God communes with the believer by agency of Holy Spirit, based on the atoning blood of his Son Jesus Christ. So today God's presence is made known to the believer by Holy Spirit. Under the New Testament, the role of the minister is to bring those he or she serves into the presence of God to equip them for service in the kingdom of God. Like the priest of the Old Testament, the unique role of the minister is to keep a little space between himself and the people so that he can hear from God and rightly represent God to the people. The space is not for celebrity status, it is for mediation between God and His people.

In the Jordan stage of ministry, ministers should have a full understanding of their role as bearers of God's presence. They should live their lives in such a way that they are able to bring those that are following them into the presence of God. They will be able to bear God's presence before the people if they spend quality time with Him and live a consecrated life of worship to God in all that they do. They should maintain a humble and loving relationship with the people and yet stay reverent towards God. Without a consecrated life of love and service to the people, a minister may still operate in the anointing of the gift but not walk in the fruit of God's love, which is the greatest of all the gifts. In fact it is love that embodies all the other fruit, so it is essential that ministers walk in love when they are not in the mode of their ministry gift. Just as there is an anointing to preach and teach the Word of God, there is also an anointing to love God's people. Loving people is just as spiritual as sharing the Word – I Corinthians 13:13, Galatians 5:22-25.

Ministers should not conduct themselves like worldly celebrities and surround themselves with body guards and build fences between themselves and the people. I realize that in some instances security and safety can put limits on interaction with the masses, but the celebrity selectivity that is observed in many cases is just a front to prevent interaction with certain people whom the minister feels are not important or do not deserve his or her attention. This type of conduct does not show the love of God and hinders the minister from truly presenting God's presence to the people. The minister should serve the people as Jesus did in His earthly ministry. He always demonstrated the love of the Father and always did His will. Like Jesus, ministers should never present themselves as being more important than those they lead, but should take advantage of every opportunity to show the love of their heavenly Father.

MERCY MEETINGS

Exodus 25:16, 20, 22

16 *And thou shalt put into the ark the testimony which I shall give thee.*

20 *And the cherubims shall stretch forth their wings on high, covering the mercy seat with their wings, and their faces shall look one to another; toward the mercy seat shall the faces of the cherubims be.*

22 *And there I will meet with thee, and I will commune with thee from above the mercy seat, from between the two cherubims which are upon the ark of the testimony, of all things which I will give thee in commandment unto the children of Israel.*

The Ark was a 4'x 2'x 2' box made of acacia wood. The top or lid of the Ark was known as the Mercy Seat. It was made of acacia wood covered with pure gold. The lid was also called a cover, denoting God's ability to cover our sin in His Mercy. It's the place where God would come to commune with the Priest. The Ark was located inside the Holy of Holies just past the Alter of Incense. Aaron, the high priest, would go there once a year to atone for the sins of the nation with the blood of a lamb.

Covenant is defined as a compact, agreement, or contract between two people, binding them mutually (equally) to an undertaking on the behalf of each other. In the Hebrew language it is call BERIT or BARA, which means bind.

God's mercy comes with His covenant. Ministers should have frequent and on-going meetings with God at His Mercy Seat so that they will find the grace to minister effectively at all times. Your frequent mercy meeting with God is a part of the covenant you have with Him. Without the grace of God, you will grow weary in well doing. Doing well will not sustain you in ministry. You will need grace and more grace, and that grace can always be obtained at the Mercy Seat of God. In God's presence you will always be refreshed and revived for ministry.

Many times ministers become so busy with kingdom's business that they neglect spending quality time with the King.

Have you had your mercy-meeting today? - Deuteronomy. 7:9, I Kings 8:23, Nehemiah 9:32, Hebrews 4:16.

WATER WALKERS

Joshua 3:12-14

12 *Now therefore take you twelve men out of the tribes of Israel, out of every tribe a man.*

13 *And it shall come to pass, as soon as the soles of the feet of the priests that bear the ark of the LORD, the LORD of all the earth, shall rest in the waters of Jordan, that the waters of Jordan shall be cut off from the waters that come down from above; and they shall stand upon an heap.*

14 *And it came to pass, when the people removed from their tents, to pass over Jordan, and the priests bearing the Ark of the Covenant before the people;*

Ministers should be the first to get into the water. They must get into the water in order to part it. When faced with a crisis of faith to cross the raging Jordan River, God told Joshua to have the Ark Bearers, the priests, to be the first to put their feet into the water. When they did, the waters of the Jordan were parted and the Israelites went across it into the Promised Land. Like the Old Testament priests, the New Testament ministers should be the first to launch out into new waters of ministry. These new waters will require faith to believe that God will part the waters once you have place your feet in it. These new waters may represent starting a church, going on the mission field, moving to a new and strange land or raising a large sum of money to finance a special project God has laid on your heart to finance.

HARVEST EVANGELISM

Joshua 3:15

And as they that bare the ark were come unto Jordan, and the feet of the priests that bare the ark were dipped in the brim of the water, (for Jordan overfloweth all his banks all the time of harvest,)

Jordan is a place of harvest. It is where the minister learns evangelism. The river speaks of the life-giving ability of God's Spirit as He flows through the land to bring growth and life for the harvest - Joshua. 3:15. While you may or may not be called to the office of an evangelist, all ministers are required to participate in the harvest of souls for the Kingdom of God. Therefore, ministers should always be sensitive to Holy Spirit's leadings in times of harvest. By practicing the presence of God, you will be in tune with Holy Spirit to harvest souls on any occasion.

Ministers should learn that harvest follows evangelism, and evangelism is brought about by the flow of the river of Holy Spirit, and Holy Spirit bring revival to those who have life. Therefore, ministers should stay in a posture of revival. Only the revived can bring life to the dead (lost). I believe that the term revival is often misused in the body of Christ. The term revive, simply means to bring to life again, or to have life again. In this context, the lost do not have life; they are in need of life. When ministers are revived they can offer the dead (lost) the life of Jesus in the love of the Father. – 1 John 4:7-9.

Ministers should keep themselves revived by staying in God presence as much as possible, because God is life and the giver of life - 1 John 1:2. When we make frequent visits to His throne of grace our lives should be revived by Holy Spirit. We are told by Jesus in John 15 to abide in Him and His love as He abides in the

Father's love. Here again I want to emphasize the importance of abiding in God's loving presence so that you will be revived with his life. It is His life that we offer to the lost. But His life should always be offered in love - 1 John 4:16; 5:12. So, when the saved are revived they can bring loving-life to the dead (lost).

STANDING FIRM

Joshua 3:16-17

16 *That the waters which came down from above stood and rose up upon an heap very far from the city Adam, that is beside Zaretan: and those that came down toward the sea of the plain, even the salt sea, failed, and were cut off: and the people passed over right against Jericho.*

17 *And the priests that bare the ark of the covenant of the LORD stood firm on dry ground in the midst of Jordan, and all the Israelites passed over on dry ground, until all the people were passed clean over Jordan.*

Jordan is the place where the minister learns to stand firmly in trouble (in the midst of troubled waters until the people pass over). Ministers should stand firm on what they believe, preach and teach. They should provide dry ground in the midst of trouble waters for those they lead. Thus, ministers should stand firm on the Word of God when it comes to social issues such as homosexuality, lesbianism, abortion, fornication, cohabitating with the opposite sex, and any other issues that are contrary to scripture.

Because of the on-going corrosion of the moral fiber of our modern society, and the constant push by the world to legalize or legitimize immoral behavior, it will be the job of the ministers to guide the church in the way of truth and godliness. They must be able to articulate to the lost, under the anointing of Holy

Spirit, God's requirements for holy living no matter what immoral behavior that is sanctioned by a worldly society.

SET- APART TO BE-A-PART

Joshua 3:5-7

5 And Joshua said to the people, "Sanctify yourselves, for tomorrow the LORD will do wonders among you."

6 Then Joshua spoke to the priests, saying, "Take up the ark of the covenant and cross over before the people." So they took up the ark of the covenant and went before the people.

7 And the LORD said to Joshua, "This day I will begin to exalt you in the sight of all Israel, that they may know that, as I was with Moses, so I will be with you.

2 Timothy 2:20-21

20 But in a great house there are not only vessels of gold and silver, but also of wood and clay, some for honor and some for dishonor.

21 Therefore if anyone cleanses himself from the latter, he will be a vessel for honor, sanctified and useful for the Master, prepared for every good work.

The word Sanctify means to separate or to set apart. Jordan is the place where the minister is sanctified or set apart to lead - Joshua 3:5-7, 2 Timothy 2:20-21. It is the place where God magnifies his chosen leaders - Joshua 3:7; 2 Kings 2:5, 13-15. The word Magnify means to make large, to expand or to increase. As you began to use your new mantle, God will authenticate your ministry by placing His anointing and favor upon you.

Since you have entered the ministry of Jesus Christ, you should realize that you have made a commitment to separate yourself to a Holy Order. Yet, this separation is more than just deciding to separate yourself from the world, because all believers should do that, but you were called by God for a specific purpose. And that purpose is to equip His people. You should understand that your calling and separation is not from the people, but to the people. Therefore, you should never consider yourself above the people but rather a servant of the people. You will not find this type of policy in the world's system. God has uniquely designed His kingdom to operate in faith by love. It is His love for the people that requires you to do what He does. You see, while He is all powerful and the master all of creation, yet He is the greatest servant of all. He serves all of His creation. Without His service the world could not operate as it does.

It is fairly common for a lot of people to say that they have been called into the ministry by God. But He chooses only those who give His calling top priority in their life to anoint with the grace to operate excellently and effectively in that calling. Yes, many are called, but few are chosen. By the fact that you have come to the Jordan stage of ministry, is a clear indication that God has called and certified you as a leader in the order of Elijah.

Although you entered ministry in a serving status, you should keep in mind that those whom God calls, He also justifies, and those whom He justifies, He also glorifies. This means that God will never forget your labor of love to others for Him, but will in due season reward you if you continue to work with a humble attitude, and be faithful until your season comes. Because you know this, you can be steadfast in your labor of love, unmovable in your precious calling and always abounding in the work of the Kingdom, because you know that your labor will not go unnoticed by God - Hebrews 6:10, 1 Peter 5:6-7, 1 Corinthians 15:58.

The Mantle of Love

Ministering under the covering of another
Follow-ship that leads to Leader-ship

WALKING IN LOVE

To walk in God's love, you must first experience His love. It is one thing to believe that God loves you, and yet another to know that He loves you. You know that God loves you when you actually experience His love without fear. Then you will know His love by experience as opposed to believing that He loves you by theory.

For years, I thought I was walking in God's love, but what I called God's love was based on my belief that He loved me. It wasn't until I actually experienced the Father's love that I really understood that my belief in His love was vastly different from experiencing His love. The reason I knew the difference between the two was because, up until I experience His love, I had been walking in fear.

If you walk with fear in your heart, you have not yet experienced God's love for you. 1 John 4:16 says that God is love and he who dwells in love dwells in God. 1 John 4:18 says that there is no fear in love; perfect love casts out fear. Fear has or allows torment. He who fears is not made perfect in love. You must realize that fear covers more than just being afraid of something or someone. One of its meanings is to have respect for God. The Bible defines this as godly fear. But the negative side of fear can dictate your motives and actions towards those with whom you have a relationship.

For instance, I had a fear of being rejected by others. I was jealous of others and was constantly competing for the top position in everything I did. I was selfish and thought only of myself. I thought that my achievements would put me in a better position than others. I had a low self-esteem and thought that my achievements would make up for it. I tended to see God through my own strengths, and by doing so, I did not recognize His love for me, nor did I impart his love to others. Instead, I offered my strength, subconsciously thinking that I was imparting His love. All of this was driven by my fear. Even though I was born again and filled with Holy Spirit, I still didn't know how to truly love because I had not experienced God's love for me.

When I came to the end of myself, after failure and more failure, with the help of other believers, I was finally able to experience God's love. My heart became tender and open to God, not on the basis of what I saw in Him, but how much He actually loved me for who I am, and not for what I could or could not do. Then suddenly in a moment of time, I came to realize that many are called but few are chosen. I came to realize that God loves me and has chosen me as his favorite son. In fact, He calls me His "Daddy's boy". Those were the words that penetrated my heart, and for the first time, I experienced the true love of God. At that very moment, I broke down and cried like a baby, from the sheer realization that He loves me and calls me His Daddy's Boy. Since then I could rest in the comfort of His love. I no longer had to fight or compete for his attention. I rest in Him and allow Him to do what I cannot do. I can import His love to others because I now have a better "grasp" of His love.

If you see yourself in this scenario, then you too, may need to experience the Father's love before you can truly walk in love. You see, the love of God is most essential to your success as a minister in His Kingdom. If you are to bring His kingdom, His very presence to others, then you must first be able to receive His love before you can impart His love. His love must be imparted in the simplicity of your humility. Your humility is the means by which His love is imparted to others.

Galatians 5:22 tells us that love encompasses all the fruit of Holy Spirit. If love encompasses all of the fruit of Holy Spirit, then it would stand to reason that we must first walk in love in order to impart to others the sub-fruit of joy and peace. So often we try to be patient with others, gentle with others and good to others, but none of this fruit will be imparted if we do not first walk in love.

You see, the Kingdom of God is one-third right-standing, one-third joy and one-third peace – Romans 14:17. Now where do you suppose right-standing, joy and peace come from? Yes, they come from God, who is love. These are the pillars of the Kingdom of God and you now have the Kingdom of God in you – Luke 17:21. Since the Kingdom is in you, you can indeed experience the love of God and then walk in that love as you impart it to others.

THREE ESSENTIALS FOR GOOD SUCCESS

In Joshua 1:8, God tells Joshua not to let the law depart from his mouth. The Law at that time referred to the first five books of the Bible and later included the writing of the prophets and certain aspects of Israel's history and literary writings. We now know that the Bible or the Word of God refers to the whole counsel of God; from the Old Testament to the New Testament. Currently in Christendom, the term "The Word" refers to the inspired Word of God that is found in the Bible. With that said, let's take a closer look at Joshua 1:8.

Again, God tells Joshua to speak His Word. A more accurate interpretation is to "recite" His Word. Then He tells him to meditate in His Word day and night and to observe to do all that is written in it. By complying with these three commands, Joshua would make his way prosperous and have good success. These three commands are also key components for being successful in ministry today.

SPEAKING THE WORD

As a minister, you should study God's Word so thoroughly that you become very well versed in it. You should be able to recite the Word with confidence and accuracy. This will require a good deal of your time initially and some of your time on a regular basis throughout your life time. You want to come to the place where you can apply the Word in any situation or circumstance you find yourself in. God's Word will be a comfort to you at all times. Holy Spirit will be able to comfort you based on the level of Word you have stored up in your spirit. Based on your Word-level, you will be able to get answers to life's questions. You will be able to gain knowledge and the understanding of how to apply that knowledge by receiving the wisdom you need from Holy Spirit. But Holy Spirit's impartation to you will be in direct proportion to your Word-level.

Once you have a repertoire and a reservoir of Word-knowledge, Holy Spirit will be able to quicken (make alive) you with the appropriate or a specific Word you need in any given moment or situation. In John 6:63, Jesus said that the Words that He speaks are Spirit and Life. In other words, God's Word can be made alive in you by Holy Spirit when you have taken the time to build a reservoir of Word-knowledge for Him to pull from. The more Word you have, the more Holy Spirit can provide you with on-the-spot wisdom for the situations or circumstances you may face. This wisdom will cause you to have pure motives toward others and to be peaceable and gentle in your interactions with them. You will also be full of mercy and the fruit of Holy Spirit, and without partiality and hypocrisy in your dealings with others - James 3:17. These are the godly attributes of a minister of the Gospel.

MEDITATING ON THE WORD

The Hebrew word for meditate is Hagah which means to read quietly or to talk to yourself as you think. It also involves reflecting on God's words and His ways, and then applying them to situations in everyday life – See Psalm 1:2-3; 63:6; 77:12; 143:5. Once I heard Bill Johnson, Pastor of Bethel Church in Redding, California, say that meditating is the opposite of worrying. If you know how to worry, then you know how to meditate. The difference is, in meditation you employ the same method or process but your focus is on the positive instead of the negative.

Another way of looking at meditation is a consecrated-way-of-thinking on or about the Word of God. When you meditate this way, you toss the Word around in your mind, looking at it from different angles. This enables you to grasp a fuller understanding of the various ways the Word can be applied. With the aid of Holy Spirit, you will see that a word or phrase or passage of scripture can bring you to a greater understanding of a single word, or the entire Bible. You will be able to juxtapose, compare, or contrast one scripture with another and come up with a revelation or insight into the mind of God or a better grasp of His Kingdom. You may get a fresh revelation about yourself or other Christians as well as how to apply the Word of God in a particular situation.

Meditating on the Word provides you with wisdom as to how to preach and teach the Word of God to others. If you make it a habit to meditate on the Word, you will never be at a loss for having something good from the Word to share. Your fresh insights on the Word will cause you to be creative in presenting the Word with originality, and in your own unique style. Most importantly, your meditation on the Word will cause you to hear directly from God. You won't have to use someone else's material and try to make it yours. When you hear directly from God, you will always have the passion and anointing to convey your message to others with boldness and authority.

OBSERVING AND DOING

The third and final essential for success in ministry is "observing to do". Joshua was told to observe to do all that God commanded him to do. The same is true for you, the minister of God. You are to observe to do all that God has commanded you to do in the Word of God, the Bible. When you observe to do, you pay close and careful attention to what God says to you. You study and thoroughly examine His instructions to you. Once you have observed what you have been told, then it is time to do what you have been told to do. You may say that this is rather simple and does not deserve the attention I am giving it here. But, you may be surprised to know that disobedience is a common problem of believers. So much so, that God made provision for it in scriptures by having James write about it in the New Testament.

James says that we should not be just hearers of the Word but doers of the Word also –James 1:21-25. You should also keep in mind that whenever we speak of the Word we are speaking about Jesus Christ, whether it is the Written-Word, which is the Logos of Jesus Christ, or the Living-Word revealed, which is the Rhema of Jesus Christ. So, when you hear or read the Word and never do the Word, you are being disobedient to Jesus Christ, your Lord and Savior. James goes on to say that you can easily deceive yourself when you hear or read the Word and don't do what the Word says. You may say how does one deceive oneself by just reading or hearing the Word and never doing the Word? James also gives us the missing ingredient here. He says that faith without works is dead – James 2:17, 20. Now we can see that our faith is employed when we obey the Word.

In Romans 10:17, Paul says that faith comes by hearing and hearing by the Word of God. If you just hear the Word and do not take corresponding action, by actually doing what the Word says, then the faith that you received to do the Word dies because you do not follow through with corresponding action. We can see that "observe to do" is the same as acting on your faith with corresponding action. The corresponding action is what consummates the faith you received when you read or hear the Word. To consummate something means to perfect or complete it. It carries the idea that something is at a supreme state or flawlessness.

Paul says in Romans 10:17 that faith comes by hearing and hearing by the Word of God. What this means is that the more attention you give to hearing, observing and examining the Word, the more you will comprehend when you hear or read the Word. This is when Holy Spirit will reveal things to you from the Word of God. This is called revelation knowledge. This is where you go beyond the mere surface of what you heard or observed to a deeper understanding, not only what you might be focused on in a particular context, but toward a deeper understanding of the entire Word of God as well.

In the absence of "observing to do" or taking the corresponding action, you are merely hearing and receiving faith but not doing anything with it. This sets up a false sense of knowledge, because this knowledge has not been substantiated by the experience of actually doing what you were told to do. You will then become deceived by your knowledge, because you are trying to replace your faith with what you know without the grace to do what you know. Your deception comes because you do not have the grace to do what you intellectually know to do. When your faith is followed by corresponding action, you will have the grace to do what you know to do. You see, the grace of God resides in His Spirit. Holy Spirit will always provide you with grace to obey the Word of God. When you obey the Word, Holy Spirit imparts grace to consummate your faith by your action – John 16:13-15.

One of the definitions for grace is divine enablement or empowerment. You can't do anything that you have not been empowered to do; not even to say yes to Jesus to receive His salvation. That is why Paul tells us in Ephesians 2:8 that we are saved by grace and not of ourselves; it is a gift from God. Just think, God gives you the grace to open your mouth to say yes to salvation, and without it you couldn't even say yes. This alone should highlight the importance of grace in consummating your faith by your actions.

Following up on what you hear or read with corresponding action brings the Old Testament concept of "observing to do" and the New Testament concept of "hearer and doer of the Word" together. Thus, by observing to do, you will be in a better position to hear Holy Spirit more clearly and thereby walk more to the center of God's will for your life. Then Holy Spirit can impart more wisdom, knowledge and understanding to you. He can then reveal to you mysteries in Christ as well as how to conduct yourself in ministry so that you will always be on point with God and man. Holy Spirit can guide you into all truth about yourself, about others around you and about ministry in general. He will guide you in your personal and corporate relationships, in your family life, in your business, and in managing your finances.

Historically, the downfall of many ministers has been in the areas of family, finances and immorality. If you employ these three essential components of success from Joshua 1:8, you will be sustained in ministry and enjoy the blessings of God and man. God's Word to you is just as it was to Joshua. When you observe to do all that He commands you to do, He will keep you from falling and present you faultless before the presence of His glory with exceedingly joy - Jude 24.

Getting God's Best in Ministry

Ministering under the covering of another
Follow-ship that leads to Leader-ship

WALKING IN HUMILITY

The Noah Webster 1928 Dictionary defines humility as freedom from pride and arrogance; humbleness of mind; a modest estimate of one's own worth. Webster's II New College Dictionary defines humble as modesty and meekness in behavior, attitude, or spirit.

There are many ways the words humility and humble can be used. For instance they can be used in the context of someone's estimation of his or her self-worth. They can be used in the context of someone being defeated or crushed. They can also be used in the context of someone choosing to submit (in attitude and behavior) to someone of greater power and authority for the purpose of being effective and getting a future reward. In this book, I am using the words humility and humble in the context of submission to God in attitude and behavior.

To be humble is not a sign of weakness but rather a godly quality. Jesus was a humble man who healed the sick, raised the dead and walked on water. If He could do those things being humble, then to be humble is a worthy state to be in. Jesus could not have done these things while walking in pride and arrogance, because God would have resisted Him. James 4:6 says that "God resists the proud but gives grace to the humble." The more humble you are, the more grace you will get from God.

So, you can see that with God's grace, you can do what Jesus did when He was on the earth. You can even do greater things than He did because you have God's Holy Spirit living inside of you; and when need be, He will come upon you to give you power to do God's will. You see, the grace of God comes by way of His Holy Spirit.

In fact, the Greek word for spirit is Pneuma and the Greek word for spiritual is Pneumatikos. The Greek word for grace is Charis and the Greek word for the grace of the spirit is Charisma. When you put Pneuma with Charis you get Charismatikos, which is the Greek word for spiritual gifts as found in 1 Corinthians 12:1.

Now we see that God's grace resides in His Holy Spirit. That is why we cannot live a spiritual life apart from the grace of God. This is one of the main reasons why we have to be born again to enter the spiritual kingdom of God – John 3:3 and Romans 14:17. When we are born again, our spirit is renewed by God's Spirit and His grace is imparted to us at that very moment. What an awesome God we serve!

If you are a bona fide Christian and do not walk in humility, it is because you do not really understand that God's grace is available so that you can. Those in Christ who do not express his humility do so because they are still carnal in their thinking. They are still operating under the world's standards and have not had their minds renewed by God's word.

I have known many Christians, including myself, who once were proud and arrogant; ready to fight for what we wanted at the drop of a hat. We did not mind lying or cheating to get our way. We did not respect authority and were rebellious towards God and man. But when we were born again, our minds were renewed by the Word of God, enabling us to walk humbly with God and man. When you look at us now, you might think that we have always been this way. When I share with my children and others about the wild things I did before I was saved, they all say to me, I can't see you ever doing that! I can't see you being that kind of person! Why do they say that? They say it because they are looking at the results of God's grace working mightily in me to bring about a godly state of humility. That is not to say that I have arrived in the area of humility. Humility is a continuous process that all Christians have to go through. But we can come to a place of being consistently humble as we grow in Christ.

In this chapter, I want to spend time with you on the subject of humility. I want to also share with you keys to humility that will help you to obtain God's best for you in ministry.

HUMILITY AND REVERENCE

Proverb 22:4
By humility and the fear of the LORD are riches, and honor, and life.

Notice, the way you get God's best in life is by two things, Humility and Fear (Reverence). Now what does humility and fear get you? They get you three things, Riches, Honor and Life. These are the three things that all people seek, the saved and the unsaved. Only, the unsaved will never obtain eternal life unless they receive Jesus Christ as Lord and Savior. Therefore, humility and the fear of the Lord are two of the most important commodities a minister should have. Now let's take a closer look at this word humility in scripture.

In Micah 6:8, God give the keys for success in His Kingdom. This verse says that God has shown you what is good. The Bible says that God is good. If you read and study the word of God you will come to know what is good, and that is God Himself. If God is good, then all that He requires you to do will be good to you and good for you. This verse says that God has also shown them what He requires of them, in that He had spoken to them previously back in Deuteronomy 10:12. Here He tells them that He requires them to fear Him, to walk in all His ways, and to love him and serve him with all their heart and soul. We find the same requirement for the New Testament ministers in Matthew 22:37; only now we have Holy Spirit to help us do it. But God chooses to simplify the matter in Micah 6:8 by saying that the requirement is to 1) do justly, 2) love mercy, and 3) walk humbly with Him. These are the three verbs of ministry.

Ministers should always do justly because they have been justified to a position of right-standing with God by the blood of His son Jesus Christ. Therefore, He expects them to do justly by Him and others.

Ministers should love mercy and come boldly to the mercy seat of God on a frequent basis to renew His mercy in them. This is simply done with a consistent prayer life. Prayer is the key to hearing from God and flowing with God every day. A minister should not start his or her day without prayer.

I believe that humility is the key to executing the three verbs of ministry: do justly, love mercy and walk humbly with God. First of all, you have to be humble to receive from God. By your humility, you make your requests to God. When you are humble, God does not resist you, but gives you more grace, which causes you to love and reverence Him more. When His love is in you, you are able to love others and walk in humility while doing so. More importantly, by your humility and reverence for God, you will obtain God's riches in the earth and in heaven. You will obtain honor in heaven and the honor of men on the earth. You will live a victorious life on earth and a celestial life in heaven that is beyond your wildest, sanctified imagination. Glory to God!

Appendix
NOTABLE EXAMPLES OF
BIBLICAL LEADERSHIP

Ministering under the covering of another
Follow-ship that leads to Leader-ship

In this section I have provided some notable examples of biblical leadership. Along with them are pointers on what to look for in a godly leader as well as characteristics of a godly leader. You will also find scripture references alongside each example, pointer or characteristic.

This is your opportunity to conduct personal research on the subject of leadership. Here you will be able to put the meat on the bones that I have provided for you. Although we have discussed at length many biblical concepts, principles and truths about follow-ship and leadership, nothing that we have discussed will be more valuable to you than your own research on the subject. I encourage you to explore the Word of God for yourself. In doing so, I am confident that God will add greater depth to what you already know.

Examples of leadership:

The greatest in the kingdom of God is the most humble - **Matthew 18:1-9; John 13:1-9**

Leadership starts with a personal revelation of who Jesus is - **Matthew 16:13**

Jesus builds your ministry upon your revelation of Him - **Matthew 16:18**

Jesus gives the keys of His kingdom to those who know him by personal revelation - **Matthew 16:19**

Jesus gives leadership authority to those who have the revelation of who he is - **Matthew 16:19, Luke 10:19, Mark 3:13-15**

What to Look for in a Godly Leader:

One who Calls others to follow and has a master plan from God - **Matthew 4:18-20**

One who motivates others to follow and has the grace (charisma) to lead - **John 1:43-47**

One who points his followers to the One he is following - **I Corinthians 11:1**

One who develops a long-standing relationship with followers - **Acts 16:1-5**

One who keeps his vision before those he is leading - **John 5:36-37**

CHARACTERISTICS OF A GODLY LEADER:

Has an acute sense of timing - **John 9:4; John 2:4; John 7:6**

Intercedes for new leadership - **Numbers 27:12-17; John 17:9-18**

God chooses his successor and reveals it to him - **I Samuel 16:11-13; I Kings 19:16; Deuteronomy 31:14**

Recognizes potential leadership qualities in those he leads - **I Kings 19:19-21**

Prepares a God-chosen follower to take his place - **I Kings 19:16; II Kings 2:1**

In closing, I want to encourage those who are in a position of leadership to look for your Elisha. Take the initiative to pull him or her under your wings. Let them know that you see their potential and are willing to help them to get to their Jordan. I want to also encourage all of you who may be in the Elisha position, to stay with your Elijah until you get clear direction from the Lord. "Learn all you can and can all you learn." As you continue to be faithful to your calling, you will get the opportunity to open and use all that you have canned.

ABOUT THE AUTHOR

Prindle House Publishing
c/o Bill Jamison
PO BOX 18761
Jacksonville, FL 32229
866-877-4635

Bill was born in Prairie, Mississippi in 1945. He was raised in a Christian home but did not commit his life to the Lord Jesus Christ until 1975. Bill is an ordained and licensed Elder and Minister of the Gospel. He is married to the former Miss Diane Elmore of Detroit, Michigan and they have seven children.

Bill has extensive experience as a Minister of the Gospel and as a Corporate Executive in the Government of the United States of America. In 1978, Bill answered the call to the ministry of the Gospel and has taught and preached the Word of God for over thirty three years. Bill's ministry gift is in the area of preaching and teaching the inspired the Word of God with a prophetic expression. He has spent the greater part of his ministry as an itinerant minister. This is evident by his extensive travel and his many associations with churches and ministries through the United State and in foreign lands. In 1999, Bill returned from the country of Iceland where he spent five year working for the U.S. Department of the Navy. During his tour in Iceland he started a church and ministered as pastor for 18 months. He also ministered as pastor of the Vineyard Christian Fellowship Church at Naval Air Station Keflavik, Iceland during the last year of his stay in Iceland. While there he ministered at many of the Icelandic Christian churches and ministered on the Icelandic Christian Television Network (ICTN). Currently, Bill is an affiliate minister at Faith Christian Center in Jacksonville, FL., where he serves as a Staff Member, Bible Teacher and an Adjunct Minister of the Gospel.

Bill is a graduate of the Word of Faith Southeastern Bible Training Center in Jacksonville, FL. He holds a Master of Human Relations Degree from the University of Oklahoma and BA Degree in Psychology from Columbia College of Missouri. He is a graduate of the Air University's Leadership and Management Development Course and is a Certified Master Instructor. He is a graduate of the Department of Defense Race Relations Institute and has extensive experience in the areas of Human Relations and Civil Rights. He is also a graduate of the Office of Civilian Personnel Management's Equal Employment Opportunity (EEO) Management Course, the EEO Counselors Course, and the EEO Law Course.

Some of Bill's noted tours of duty have been with the U.S. Air Force, from 1965 to 1980, where he served both as a noncommissioned officer and a civilian employee in the Social Actions Program. From 1980 to 1985, he served with the Department of Energy as a Project Manager of Energy Conservation Programs. Bill went to work for the Department of Navy in October 1989 and served as Deputy EEO Officer for Naval Air Station, Meridian until October 1993. He served as the Deputy EEO Officer for Naval Air Station in Keflavik, Iceland form October 1993 to January 1999. From February 1999 to December 2003, Bill served as the Affirmative Employment Manager; an Ombudsman; a Complaint Manager; an EEO Counselor and Senior EEO Specialist at the Federal Law Enforcement Training Center in Brunswick, GA. He retired from federal service in 2003 and has since been ministering and writing Christian books and articles.